SHEPHERD'S NOTES

D1202527

SHEPHERD'S NOTES

When you need a guide through the Scriptures

Psalms 51~100

BROADMAN
&HOLMAN
PUBLISHERS

Nashville, Tennessee

Shepherd's Notes®—*Psalms 51–100*
© 1999
by Broadman & Holman Publishers
Nashville, Tennessee
All rights reserved
Printed in the United States of America

0–8054–9340–9
Dewey Decimal Classification: 223.207
Subject Heading: BIBLE. O.T. PSALMS
Library of Congress Card Catalog Number: 99–11544

Library of Congress Cataloging-in-Publication Data

Gould, Dana, 1951–
Psalms 51–100 / Dana Gould, editor [i.e. author].
    p. cm. — (Shepherd's notes)
    Includes bibliographical references.
    ISBN 0–8054–9340–9 (pbk.)
    1. Bible. O.T. Psalms LI-C—Study and teaching.   I. Title.   II. Title: Psalms
fifty-one to one hundred. III. Series
  BS1430.5.G682   1999
  223'.207—dc21   99–11544
                                                CIP

1 2 3 4 5   03 02 01 00 99

CONTENTS

Dear Reader:

Shepherd's Notes are designed to give you a quick, step-by-step overview of every book of the Bible. They are not meant to be substitutes for the biblical text; rather, they are study guides intended to help you explore the wisdom of Scripture in personal or group study and to apply that wisdom successfully in your own life.

Shepherd's Notes guide you through the main themes of each book of the Bible and illuminate fascinating details through appropriate commentary and reference notes. Historical and cultural background information brings the Bible into sharper focus.

Six different icons, used throughout the series, call your attention to historical-cultural information, Old Testament and New Testament references, word pictures, unit summaries, and personal application for everyday life.

Whether you are a novice or a veteran at Bible study, I believe you will find *Shepherd's Notes* a resource that will take you to a new level in your mining and applying the riches of Scripture.

In Him,

David R. Shepherd
Editor-in-Chief

DESIGNED FOR THE BUSY USER

Shepherd's Notes for Psalms 51–100 is designed to provide an easy-to-use tool for getting a quick handle on this portion of this significant Bible book's important features, and for gaining an understanding of its messages. Information available in more difficult-to-use reference works has been incorporated into the *Shepherd's Notes* format. This brings you the benefits of many advanced and expensive works packed into one small volume.

Shepherd's Notes are for laymen, pastors, teachers, small-group leaders and participants, as well as the classroom student. Enrich your personal study or quiet time. Shorten your class or small-group preparation time as you gain valuable insights into the truths of God's Word that you can pass along to your students or group members.

DESIGNED FOR QUICK ACCESS

Bible students with time constraints will especially appreciate the timesaving features built into the *Shepherd's Notes*. All features are intended to aid a quick and concise encounter with the heart of the messages of Psalms 51–100.

Concise Commentary. Short sections provide quick "snapshots" of the themes of the psalms.

Outlined Text. Comprehensive outlines cover the entire text of Psalms 51–100. This is a valuable feature for following each psalm's flow, allowing for a quick, easy way to locate a particular passage.

Shepherd's Notes. These summary statements or capsule thoughts appear at the close of every key section of the psalms. While functioning in part as a quick summary, they also deliver the essence of the message presented in the sections which they cover.

Icons. Various icons in the margin highlight recurring themes in Psalms 51–100, aiding in selective searching or tracing of those themes.

Questions to Guide Your Study. These thought-provoking questions and discussion starters are designed to encourage interaction with the truth and principles of God's Word.

DESIGNED TO WORK FOR YOU

Personal Study. Using the *Shepherd's Notes* with a passage of Scripture can enlighten your study and take it to a new level. At your fingertips is information that would require searching several volumes to find. In addition, many points of application occur throughout the volume, contributing to personal growth.

Teaching. Outlines frame the text of Psalms 51–100, providing a logical presentation of their messages. Capsule thoughts designated as "Shepherd's Notes" provide summary statements for presenting the essence of key points and events. Application icons point out personal application of the messages of the psalms. Historical Context icons indicate where cultural and historical background information is supplied.

Group Study. *Shepherd's Notes* can be an excellent companion volume to use for gaining a quick but accurate understanding of the messages of Psalms 51–100. Each group member can benefit from having his or her own copy. The *Note's* format accommodates the study of themes throughout Psalms 51–100. Leaders may use its flexible features to prepare for group sessions or use them during group sessions. Questions to guide your study can spark discussion of Psalms 51–100's key points and truths to be discovered in these profound psalms.

LIST OF MARGIN ICONS USED IN PSALMS 51–100

 Shepherd's Notes. Placed at the end of each section, a capsule statement provides the reader with the essence of the message of that section.

 Historical Context. To indicate background information—historical, biographical, cultural—and provide insight on the understanding or interpretation of a passage.

 Old Testament Reference. Used when the writer refers to Old Testament passages or when Old Testament passages illuminate a text.

 New Testament Reference. Used when the writer refers to New Testament passages that are either fulfilled prophecy, an antitype of an Old Testament type, or a New Testament text which in some other way illuminates the passages under discussion.

 Personal Application. Used when the text provides a personal or universal application of truth.

 Word Picture. Indicates that the meaning of a specific word or phrase is illustrated so as to shed light on it.

The book of Psalms or the *Psalter* is the hymnal of Israelite worship and the Bible's book of personal devotions. In it we not only find expression of all the emotions of life but also some of the most profound teaching in the entire Bible.

DATE AND AUTHORSHIP OF THE PSALMS

The Psalter was not completed until late in Israelite history (in the postexilic era). But it contains hymns written over a period of hundreds of years.

Evidence of the superscriptions. A primary source of information regarding the date and authorship of individual psalms are the superscriptions found above many psalms. According to these, some of the authors include David, the sons of Korah, Asaph, Moses, and Solomon. Other psalms, including some of the "Psalms of Ascent" (Pss. 120–134) and "Hallelujah" psalms (Pss. 146–150) are anonymous. These superscriptions, if taken at face value, would date many of the psalms to the early tenth century (psalms of David) and at least one to the fifteenth century (Ps. 90).

Meaning and reliability of the superscriptions. Some scholars, however, question whether the superscriptions are meant to ascribe authorship to the Psalms. A more serious question is whether the superscriptions are reliable. Some scholars believe they were added at a late date and are no more than conjectures that have no real historical value. But there are good reasons to believe the superscriptions can be trusted.

The phrase *ledawid* used frequently in the psalm superscriptions could mean "by David" or "for David." But the clause following the superscription to Psalm 18 favors "by David."

Many of the psalm superscriptions refer to incidents in the life of David about which Samuel and Chronicles say nothing. For example, the superscription of Psalm 60 mentions battles with Aram-Naharaim, Aram-Zobah, and Edom. It would be strange if, in the late postexilic period, rabbis invented this. Another example is the superscription of Psalm 7, which speaks of a certain "Cush the Benjamite" (he is mentioned only here in the Old Testament). If the superscriptions were late fabrications, one would expect that they would refer more to incidents from David's life mentioned in Samuel.

Many of the psalm superscriptions contain technical musical terms, the meanings of which were already lost by the time the Old Testament was translated into Greek. For example, *lammenasseah*, the word which means "for the choir leader," is wrongly translated "to the end" in the Septuagint, the pre-Christian Greek translation of the Old Testament. A number of these terms are still not understood.

Obscure or difficult words in the superscriptions include:

- *Song Titles:* "Do Not Destroy"; "A Dove on Distant Oaks"; "The Doe of the Morning"; "Lilies"; "The Lilies of the Covenant"; and "Mahalath"
- *Musical Instruments* or *Technical Terms:* "stringed instruments" and "Sheminith"
- *Musical Guilds* or *Singers:* "Asaph"; "Sons of Korah"; "Heman the Ezrahite"; "Ethan the Ezrahite"
- *Types of Psalms:* "Songs of Ascent," likely sung by those who were making a pilgrimage to Jerusalem; *maskil,* possibly an instructional or meditative psalm.

Ancient terminology and references to old guilds and bygone events all imply that the titles are very old. This supports confidence in their reliability.

Davidic authorship of Psalms. Many scholars have asserted that David did not write the Psalms attributed to him. But there are no historical reasons why David could not have authored those Psalms. David had a reputation as a singer and as a devoted servant of the Lord, and nothing in his life is incompatible with his being a psalmist.

One difficulty that has been raised is that some of the Psalms of David seem to refer to the Temple (for example, 27:4), which did not exist in his day. But terms like "house of the Lord," "holy place," and "house of God" are regularly used of the tent of meeting and need not be taken as references to Solomon's Temple (see Exod. 28:43; 29:30; Josh. 6:24).

Other psalms that mention the Temple, however, are also ascribed to David (Pss. 5; 11; 18; 27; 29; 65; 68; 138). The word *temple* (*hêkal*) does not necessarily refer to Solomon's Temple. The word *hêkal* is used in 1 Samuel 1:9; 3:3 of the tabernacle. It also refers sometimes to God's dwelling place as in 2 Samuel 22:7. In Psalm 27 God's house is called "house," "temple," "booth," and "tent."

The date of the Psalms. Earlier critics dated many of the Psalms late in Israel's history, some as late as the Maccabean period. For two reasons, however, this is no longer possible.

First, the Ugaritic songs and hymns show parallels to many of the Psalms. The grammar and poetic forms are similar. The Ugaritic tradition of hymn writing is ancient (before the twelfth

Ugarit was an important city in Syria whose excavation has provided tablets giving closest primary evidence available for reconstructing the Canaanite religion that was a perennial temptation to Israel.

century B.C.) and implies that many of the Psalms may be ancient too.

Second, a fragmentary, second-century B.C. copy of the biblical collection of Psalms was found in the Dead Sea Scrolls. This proves beyond doubt that the Psalms were composed well before the second century B.C., since it must have taken a long time for the written Psalms to be recognized as Scripture and for the Psalter to be organized.

There is no reason, therefore, to date all the Psalms late. Generally speaking, they can be dated to three broad periods: (1) *Preexilic.* This would include those Psalms that are very much like the Ugaritic songs, the royal psalms, and those that mention the Northern Kingdom. (2) *Exilic.* This would include the dirge songs that lament the fall of Jerusalem and call for vengeance on the Edomites and others. (3) *Early postexilic.* This would include Psalms that emphasize the written Law, such as Psalm 119.

THE COMPILATION OF THE PSALMS

Psalms divides into five sections or "books":

Book One:	Psalms 1–41
Book Two:	Psalms 42–72
Book Three:	Psalms 73–89
Book Four:	Psalms 90–106
Book Five:	Psalms 107–150

We have no precise information regarding the dates when the five books of the Psalms were compiled or what the criteria of compilation were. Psalm 72:20 implies that a compilation of David's psalms was made shortly after his death.

In Hezekiah's time there were collections of the psalms of David and Asaph, which may account for the bulk of the first three books (2 Chron. 29:30). At a later date another scribe may have collected the remaining books of the Psalter. Psalms was put into its final form some time in the postexilic period.

The five books each close with a doxology, and Psalm 150 is a concluding doxology for the entire Psalter. But the numbering of the Psalms varies. The Jerusalem Talmud speaks of 147 psalms. The Septuagint divides Psalms 116 and 147 into two psalms each but numbers Psalms 9 and 10 and Psalms 114 and 115 as one psalm each.

King Hezekiah and his officials ordered the Levites to praise the Lord with the words of David and of Asaph the seer. So they sang praises with gladness and bowed their heads and worshiped (2 Chron. 29:30).

TYPES OF PSALMS

When studying a psalm, one should ask the following questions: (1) Was it sung by an individual or the congregation? (2) What was the psalm's purpose (praise, cry for help, thanksgiving, admonition)? (3) Does it mention any special themes, such as the royal house or Zion? By asking these questions, scholars have identified a number of psalm types.

Hymns. In this type of psalm, the whole congregation praises God for His works or attributes (Ps. 105). Six subcategories of hymns are:

Victory songs, which praise God for His victories over the nations (Ps. 68);

Processional hymns, sung as the worshipers moved into the Temple area (Ps. 24);

Zion songs, which praise God and specifically refer to His presence in Zion (Ps. 48);

Songs of the *Lord's reign,* which include the words, "The LORD reigns" (Ps. 99);

Antiphonal hymns chanted by either the priests or choir with the congregation responding antiphonally (Ps. 136); and

Hallelujah hymns, which begin or end with "Praise the LORD!" (Hebrew, *hallelu Yah;* Ps. 146).

Community complaints. In these psalms the whole nation voiced its complaints over problems it was facing, such as defeat in battle, famine, or drought (Ps. 74). A subcategory of this is the *national imprecation,* in which the people cursed their oppressors as enemies of Israel's God (Ps. 83).

Individual complaints. These psalms are like the community complaint except that they were prayers given by one person instead of the whole nation. The reason for the prayers might be that the individual was sick, hounded by enemies, or in need of confessing personal sin (Ps. 13). This type of psalm may include substantial *imprecation* or curses against the psalmist's personal enemies (Ps. 5). A subcategory is the *penitential psalm,* in which the speaker is dominated by a sense of guilt (Ps. 51).

Individual songs of thanksgiving. In these psalms an individual praises God for some saving act. Usually it alludes to a time that the individual was sick or in some other kind of trouble (Ps. 116).

Royal psalms. These psalms deal with the king and the royal house. Subcategories include:

Wedding songs, sung at the marriage of the king (Ps. 45);

Coronation songs (Ps. 72);

Prayers for victory, chanted when the king went to war (Ps. 20); and

Votive psalms, perhaps sung by the king at his coronation as a vow to be faithful and upright (Ps. 101).

Torah psalms. These psalms give moral or religious instruction (Pss. 1; 127). Subcategories include:

Testimony songs in which the psalmist used his personal experience of God's salvation to encourage the hearer (Ps. 32); and

Wisdom songs, in which the psalmist instructed the hearer more in practical wisdom similar to that in Proverbs than in the law (Ps. 49).

Oracle psalms. These psalms report a decree of God (Ps. 82). The content of the oracle is often divine judgment, and the psalm concludes with a prayer for God to carry out His decree. But see also Psalm 87, an oracle of salvation for the Gentiles.

Blessing psalms. In these psalms a priest pronounces a blessing upon the hearer(s) (Ps. 128).

Taunt songs. These psalms reproach the godless for their vile behavior and promise that their doom is near (Ps. 52).

Songs of trust. In these psalms the psalmist may face difficulty but remains assured of God's help and proclaims his faith and trust (Ps. 11).

When interpreting a psalm, it is important first to determine what kind of psalm it is. In this way one can see how the psalmist intended it to be read.

Torah is a Hebrew word normally translated "law" which eventually became a title for the Pentateuch, the first five books of the Old Testament.

THEOLOGICAL SIGNIFICANCE OF THE PSALMS

The Psalms help today's believers to understand God, themselves, and their relationship to God. The Psalms picture God as the Creator, who is worthy of praise and is capable of using His creative might to rescue His people from current distress. The Psalms picture God as the just Judge of all the world who rewards the righteous and opposes the wicked.

Prayers that God should curse the enemies of the psalmist must be understood in part as affirmations of God's justice and the certainty of His judgment. The Psalms picture God as the faithful friend of the oppressed. The Psalms offer a refresher course in God's faithfulness throughout Israel's history. The Psalms highlight God's promises to David and his descendants, promises that are not finally realized until Christ.

The Psalms picture the full range of human emotions: joy, despair, guilt, consolation, love, hate, thankfulness, and dissatisfaction. The Psalms thus remind us that all of life is under God's lordship. The Psalms likewise illustrate the broad range of human responses to God: praise, confession, pleas for help, thanksgiving. The Psalms thus serve as a sourcebook for Christian worship, both public and private.

THE FAITH OF THE PSALMS

As noted, the Psalms set forth the basic faith of the Hebrew people. God and man are the two basic focal points of that faith. These were the two inescapable realities. A religion which loses sight of either has failed to meet human needs. Their ancient faith also had two basic emphases: human need and divine providence. The Hebrew people were overwhelmingly aware

John Calvin called the Psalms "An Anatomy of Parts of the Soul." Calvin says, "There is not an emotion of which anyone can be conscious that is not here represented as in a mirror. Or, rather, the Holy Spirit has here drawn to the life all the griefs, sorrows, fears, doubts, hopes, cares, perplexities, in short, all the distracting emotions with which the minds of men are wont to be agitated." Calvin goes on to say that here we see God's servants laying open to God their inner thoughts and affections. The Psalms call us to lay before God all of our infirmities and vices.

that the plight of humanity was quite desperate as they faced the problems of sin, guilt, and evil. They were equally certain that God was sovereign, His purposes were good, and He would ultimately be victorious. The consequences of the divine sovereignty brought to the hearts and the lips of the Hebrews both praise and thanksgiving. They praised God for what He was and thanked Him for what He had done.

Finally, the faith of the psalmists can be characterized as having four dimensions. They always looked back to the past, to God's great acts of creation and more especially to His great acts of redemption and deliverance. In the present dimension of their faith, they were aware that God was with them, even when they did not "feel" His presence. Where they were, He was. Because of what God had done and because of their present experience with Him, they could look forward to being in His presence in the future. This gave them hope. The fourth dimension to the faith of the psalmists was timelessness. Their faith transcended time and speaks to the hearts of all people everywhere. This makes the book of Psalms a universal favorite among people. Wherever we are in our spiritual pilgrimage, we can find psalms which express our deepest thoughts, our greatest hopes, and our utmost certainties.

THE PSALMS FOR BELIEVERS TODAY

The list of teachings we gain from Psalms has no end. Its 150 songs call us to pray, to praise, to confess, and to testify. The prayer path to God is open at all times for all people in all situations. At all times we should take our feelings to God. He hears and accepts us. In His own way He answers. He brings salvation to our lives. Sin plagues each of us. We rebel against God's way.

God waits for us to confess our sins. He does not give us our deserts.

He forgives, redeems, and renews our lives. We may not be able to sing. We can praise God. We need to be aware of the great acts He is accomplishing in our lives and the great things He has accomplished for us in creation and in His saving actions through Jesus Christ. Knowing He acts for us, we can rejoice and praise Him at all times. We have no monopoly on God. He has chosen to help all nations praise Him. We must daily testify to others what God has done for us.

PSALM 51: A PLEA FOR PARDON

Background: The setting for this psalm is the prophet Nathan's visit to King David and the king's subsequent repentance (2 Sam. 12:1–23).

Theme: Repentance and forgiveness

Reader insights: A penitential psalm. This kind of psalm is a subcategory of the individual lament, in which the speaker is dominated by a sense of guilt.

PSALM SUMMARY

A plea for pardon (51:1–4). David recognized God's justice and God's grace. He acknowledged that God's view of his sin was correct and that God was the One against whom he had sinned. Nevertheless, he asked that God be gracious to him by removing his transgressions, washing him and cleansing him.

The context of sin (51:5). The psalmist acknowledged personal responsibility for his sin. He realized that his sin was a violation of God's law. He also recognized the context of his sin. All people are born into sin. We acquire a sinful nature at birth. Individually and collectively, we are all guilty before God.

*A prayer for forgiveness (51:6–12).*The repentant psalmist prayed for God's mercy and forgiveness and asked to be restored. His prayer revealed a truly repentant attitude.

A promise to share (51:13–19). The psalmist recognized that he could be effective in bringing others to God only if God cleansed him.

■ *This psalm reflects the seriousness of sin, the*
■ *pain of guilt, and the joy of repentance and*
■ *restoration. A saint is a sinner who has*
■ *repented.*

GUIDING QUESTIONS
What is the great theme of this psalm? What is generally regarded to be its background?

PSALM 52: THE BOASTFUL WICKED

Theme: Vain trust in wealth versus trust in God

Reader insights: A taunt song. This kind of psalm reproaches the godless for their vile behavior and promises that their doom is near.

PSALM SUMMARY
The "mighty man" (52:1–7). The psalmist asked why the "mighty man" brags about his wickedness (v. 1). This describes a person who uses his power in a ruthless manner. He is guilty of the sins of a sharp tongue, delighting in lies and

We see three specific words for *sin* in these two verses: iniquity, transgressions, sin.

Iniquity is a powerful word which means "perverse and crooked." It describes fallen human nature, people apart from God.

Transgressions are actions known to be in defiance of what is right. The word means "deliberate rebellion."

Sin literally means "missing the mark" or moral failure.

Background: The title of this psalm refers to the account in 1 Samuel 22.

destructive words (vv. 2–4). This man has hurt others with his tongue. The psalmist described his tongue as that which "plots destruction." It is like a "sharpened razor."

The psalmist predicted peril for the ungodly. They will be broken down and uprooted (v. 5). They will become a laughingstock because they made riches and not God their refuge (vv. 6–7).

The godly person (52:8–9). The psalmist next contrasted the righteous with the mighty man. The psalmist and others who trust in the Lord are blessed. They will flourish like an olive tree planted near the Temple (v. 8). The righteous trust in God's unfailing love, express their thanksgiving, and share their faith (v. 9).

- *The psalmist contrasted the righteous with*
- *the "mighty man." Those whose trust is in*
- *wealth will experience everlasting ruin.*
- *Those who trust in God will flourish.*

GUIDING QUESTION
What is the key contrast of this psalm?

Background: This a reflective psalm that describes the lot of God's people in a godless world.

PSALM 53: THE FOOL

Theme: A meditation about the fool

Reader insights: An oracle psalm. This psalm and Psalm 14 appear to be two versions of the same psalm that describe the sinfulness of mankind.

PSALM SUMMARY

The "fool" (53:1–4). The "fool" described in this psalm is not intellectually deficient but morally lacking. A fool may be smart and even clever. A modern description would be of secular persons—those who live without regard for God. Their lack of belief affects their behavior (vv. 2–4).

God will judge (53:5–6). Those who live without regard for God will experience His judgment—a time of terror. The psalm closes with a prayer that God will provide salvation for His captive people from out of Jerusalem.

- *God will judge those people who live with no*
- *regard for Him. But the believer may find*
- *refuge in God.*

GUIDING QUESTION

What does the psalmist mean by a "fool"?

PSALM 54: "SAVE ME, O GOD"

Theme: Faith in God during times of trouble

Reader insights: An individual lament

PSALM SUMMARY

A prayer for rescue (54:1–3). The psalmist cried out to God to rescue him. Ruthless men were threatening his life, and he prayed to be saved from them.

Anticipation of deliverance (54:4–7). The psalmist was confident that God would help him (v. 4).

Background: This prayer for deliverance is both a cry for help and a confession of David's confidence in God. The background referred to in the title is found in 1 Samuel 23:15–21. The treachery of the Ziphites is described in 1 Samuel 23:19–23; 26:1.

"Your name"

God's name is a reference to His character. In this passage, the psalmist has in mind God's character as the Judge of the wicked and the defender of the oppressed.

His enemies would be punished, and he would be vindicated. Out of gratitude he anticipated bringing "a freewill offering" to the Lord (v. 6).

- *David was confident of his enemies, punish-*
- *ment and of his own vindication. In anticipa-*
- *tion of God's help, he brought "a freewill*
- *offering" to God.*

GUIDING QUESTION
What does the psalmist mean when he uses the phrase "your name"?

Psalm 54 is often read on Good Friday. God vindicated Jesus by the Resurrection, showing that the charges of His enemies were false.

PSALM 55: ON THE WINGS OF A DOVE

Theme: God is our sure refuge in times of trouble.

Reader insights: An individual lament

PSALM SUMMARY
The psalmist longs to escape (55:1–8). This harsh lament is also a moving personal prayer. The psalmist cried out for God to hear him. Pressure from enemies was producing in him some negative emotions: anguish, terror, and the kind of fear that makes a person shake.

Background: Two traditional views have been offered. Some see this psalm as being composed during the conspiracy of David's son, Absalom, when David was driven from Jerusalem. Others see it as referring to the time when Saul was persecuting David.

One reaction to this level of stress is to get away—to fly away like a dove (vv. 6–7). There he might be safe from the storm of trouble (v. 8). The fantasy of escape may serve as an emotional safety valve, but it is not the answer to our deepest need in times of trouble.

The psalmist lashes out (55:9–15, 20–21, 23). The psalmist next turned on his enemies with a vengeance. His initial desire for flight now turned to fight. He fought back, but struck out. The poet was afflicted by his enemies and he cursed them (vv. 9–11).

Confusion of tongues in verse 9 may be a reflection of the experience of the race at the Tower of Babel (Gen. 11:5–9).

However, the hardest thing the psalmist faced was the betrayal of his friend (vv. 13–14, 20–21). The two of them had been close, sharing precious conversation and even worship of God (v. 14). All the while his friend's words had been "smooth as butter," covering the hostility in his heart.

The betrayal of his friend has cut him to the quick. He asked God to reward his enemies for their treachery (vv. 15, 23).

The psalmist takes his burden to the Lord (55:16–19, 22). Here we see the turning point of the psalm. The psalmist is now convinced that God's grace and power will cause him to be delivered from his distress.

"Cast your cares"

Cast means "to throw or fling" something. The object of this casting is our "cares." The word *cares* is variously translated "burden" or "lot." It is that package of cares and anxieties that we are each assigned in this life, however difficult they may be.

The climax of the psalm is verse 22, where we see the psalmist's ultimate trust in God. He demonstrated trust by casting his cares on the Lord, knowing God would sustain him.

■ *The psalmist was under great stress. His first*
■ *reaction was to flee. Then he wanted to*
■ *attack the source of his distress. Finally, he*
■ *yielded himself and his distress to God.*

GUIDING QUESTION

When we cast our cares upon God, what does He do for us?

PSALM 56:
TRUST IN GOD

Theme: Faith in God's care and protection

Reader insights: An individual lament. Here we have a mixture of lament over the psalmist's enemies and the confession of his faith in God.

PSALM SUMMARY

Appeal for gracious help (56:1–7). The psalmist was oppressed, trampled by his enemies. In such peril he realized he was beyond mere human help (v. 4*b*). In a memorable text he declared that when he was afraid, he would trust God (v. 3).

The psalmist's enemies were lurking and ruthless; they were out to get him (vv. 5–6). He described their evil activities and his dangerous situation. He asked that God repay them for their crimes (v. 7).

God knows what we suffer (56:8–13). It is a comfort for all believers to know that God is aware of the burdens we bear. Here the psalmist painted a lovely picture of God's awareness. God kept count of the psalmist's sleepless nights. He even saved the psalmist's tears in a bottle!

No wonder he confessed his faith, "God is for me" (v. 9). Therefore, he trusted in the Lord (v. 11), praised Him (v. 10), and brought his "thank offerings" (v. 12). It was the Lord who kept him safe and delivered him from danger (v. 13). The psalmist refused to place his confidence in human help. Like him, we may confidently place our trust in God and in the promises of His Word.

Background: David was on the run from Saul. He sought asylum with King Achish of Gath. But David learned that the king's advisors didn't like his being in their territory. He was afraid of what they might do to him.

- *The psalmist confessed his faith in God. It*
- *was God, not man who kept him safe and*
- *delivered him from danger.*

GUIDING QUESTION
What pictures did the psalmist use to show that God is aware of our difficulties?

PSALM 57: IN THE LION'S DEN

Theme: A plea for help and a prayer of praise

Reader insights: An individual lament. This psalm's twin themes—a plea for help and a prayer of praise—are tied together by the psalmist's confession of his faith.

Background: David was hiding in a cave as he fled from Saul's persecution.

PSALM SUMMARY
The psalmist's trust in the midst of enemies (57:1–6). The psalmist's faith is apparent, as he cried out for God's mercy and help. He believed that God would save him from his enemies whom he compared to lions with sharp teeth. He was prey to these fierce enemies, as they cut his reputation to pieces with their slander and false accusations.

These enemies were also cunning hunters, setting a snare and digging a pit for him—only to fall into it themselves (v. 6).

The psalmist's faith in the midst of fear (57:7–11). The psalmist sang of his steadfast faith in verse 7. He was unshaken despite the danger he faced. He could sing even in the midst of trouble. The

Christians also face an enemy—Satan and his host of demons (1 Pet. 5:8). Peter tells us that Satan is "like a roaring lion looking for someone to devour." The wise believer stays on guard against the wiles of the devil.

psalmist called for nature to awake and rejoice with him. He even went out to awaken the dawn (it usually awakens us). His joy was so complete that he could not wait for daylight to share it—like a proud father whose child has been born during the night. His thanksgiving was too good to keep to himself (v. 9). The faithfulness and love of God called forth his praise. He exalted the Lord and ascribed glory to Him "over all the earth" (v. 11).

- *The psalmist found himself in the midst of*
- *powerful enemies out to destroy him with*
- *their slander and false accusations. The*
- *psalmist was unshaken despite the danger he*
- *faced. In fact, he could sing even in the midst*
- *of trouble. In gratitude, he lifted his heart in*
- *praise.*

GUIDING QUESTION
What did the psalmist do in the midst of his enemies?

PSALM 58: JUDGE OF PEOPLE AND ANGELS

Background: The psalmist's fiery indignation against unjust judges and evildoers likely came from a heart lacerated by the sight of widespread corruption rather than from inflicted personal wrongs.

Theme: Denunciation and judgment of those who misuse authority or unfairly administer justice

Reader insights: An individual lament

PSALM SUMMARY
A call for justice (58:1–2). The psalmist denounced these unfair rulers with righteous

indignation. These unjust rulers were dealing out violence. The picture is that of *scales*, an instrument for fair dealing. Wicked men were using the scales for the purpose of doing violence to the innocent.

Wicked persons (58:3–5). It appeared to the psalmist that these rulers were bent on evil from their birth (v. 3). They were like deaf cobras who could not be controlled by the snake charmer's spell. Their venom was slander and lies.

A sevenfold curse (58:6–9). The number *seven* in Scripture stands for perfection or completeness. The psalmist pronounced a vivid sevenfold curse on the wicked rulers.

The righteous rejoice (58:10–11). God brought vengeance upon the wicked to the delight of the righteous. Verse 10 paints a gory scene. The point is that all the world will one day meet its Judge, and justice will prevail. The psalm comes to a climax in verse 11. No matter how long it takes for judgment to come, the righteous will be rewarded.

■ *God's judgment upon the wicked is inevita-*
■ *ble. God will bring vengeance upon the*
■ *wicked and reward the righteous.*

GUIDING QUESTION
Describe the psalmist's sevenfold curse. What did he ask God to do?

PSALM 59: PRAYER FOR DELIVERANCE

Theme: Divine deliverance from danger

Reader insights: An individual lament

Background: This psalm is assigned to the time when David was being pursued by Saul.

PSALM SUMMARY

A plea for deliverance (59:1–9). The psalmist petitioned God to deliver him from his enemies. "Deliver me from my enemies, . . . deliver me from evildoers" (vv. 1–2). The psalmist prayed for divine deliverance, asserting his own innocence (v. 3b). Then he called on the Almighty to "arise" to punish them (vv. 4–5). His enemies are graphically portrayed as a pack of wild dogs: howling, prowling, and snarling against him (vv. 6–7). They think they are so powerful, but they amuse the Almighty. He laughs at them (v. 8).

God is David's fortress. The refrain occurs in verse 9 (and a variation of it in v. 17): "O my Strength, I watch for you; you, O God, are my fortress, my loving God."

A prayer for help (59:10–17). In verse 11 David asked that God not slay his enemies, but let them remain as a lesson to the righteous. But then his sense of outraged justice flared into a prayer for their destruction: "Consume them in wrath, consume them till they are no more" (v. 13). These two verses are not to be taken as contradictory. Most likely the psalmist is indicating that after his enemies have served as a living example of divine retribution, he desires that God will adopt whatever measures are necessary to prevent these enemies from working their evil again. In contrast to his enemies, the confident psalmist praised God's power and protection (vv. 16–17). God's love is his fortress and refuge. He can always depend on the Lord.

- David asked God not to slay his enemies but
- to let them remain as a lesson to the righ-
- teous. Then he prayed that God would
- adopt whatever measures were necessary to
- prevent these enemies from working their
- evil again.

GUIDING QUESTION

What lessons can we draw from this psalm for our spiritual benefit today?

PSALM 60: A NATION'S PRAYER

Theme: A nation lamenting after a military defeat

Reader insights: A community lament. This oracle found in verses 6–8 is repeated in Psalm 108:7–9.

PSALM SUMMARY

The king's complaint (60:1–5). The nation has experienced defeat in battle. This was taken as a sure sign of God's rejection and anger (v. 1). The psalmist next described the effect this defeat was having on the people (vv. 2–3). They were reeling from drinking the cup of judgment.

The oracle of God (60:6–8). God's anger is formidable, but it is not final (v. 1). He still loves Israel. He promised to restore the nation and subdue their rebellious neighboring lands. The psalm pictures God as a giant warrior. He will

Background: Israel had suffered a military defeat and felt rejected by God. The occasion may be that described in 1 Samuel 8:1–14. However, this poem was probably read by the king or some other military leader at other times as well, when God failed to march "with our armies" (Ps. 60:10). This psalm is similar to Psalm 44. This is the last of the psalms with a historical setting from the life of David.

extend His control over countries on both sides of the Jordan River. He will make Ephraim, the most powerful tribe, His helmet. Judah, King David's tribe, will become His scepter (v. 7).

Like a warrior returning from battle, God will wash His hands in the Dead Sea (in the land of Moab) and toss His shoes onto Edom. He will shout victory over the plains of Philistia (in the west). This was an early representation of the kingdom of God or His rule, which was later expanded in the New Testament.

A prayer for God's help (60:9–12). The leader prayed for the safety of a fortress city such as Petra in Edom (v. 9). He asked divine help "for the help of man is worthless" (v. 11). With God's help they can defeat their enemies (v. 12). Thus, the psalm concludes on the glad note of expected victory. This psalm reinforces the truth of God's sovereign power. He is in control of human destiny—then and now.

Lessons in living: The time following a defeat is one of vulnerability. When we suffer defeats in our lives, we must be careful not to let down our guard. For that is when our enemy, Satan, stands poised and ready to attack again.

- *The nation experienced defeat in battle. They*
- *were overwhelmed and shaken. This was*
- *taken as a sure sign of God's rejection and*
- *anger. The leader prayed for God's help. With*
- *His help they could defeat their enemies.*

GUIDING QUESTION

What positive effect does God's anger have in the lives of His people?

PSALM 61: LEAD ME TO THE ROCK

Background: This petition for restoration was made by a person possibly in exile. Some assign this psalm to the period of Absalom's revolt against his father David.

Theme: Trust in God's strength and protection

Reader insights: A song of trust. This is taken by some commentators to be a royal prayer.

PSALM SUMMARY

The king's prayer (61:1–3). The king's petition was to be heard "from the ends of the earth" (vv. 1–2). Some take this to mean the psalmist was in exile. Others think the phrase means that he was near death. Most likely the reference is not geographical but spiritual. The psalmist was "at the end of his rope" and was experiencing the feeling of God's absence. Thus he prayed that God would lead him to the rock that is higher. This could be a reference to Mount Moriah on which the Temple was built. But a better interpretation is that the rock is God Himself (see Ps. 18:2). This rock was too high for the psalmist to climb, and he could reach this rock only with God's help.

Recalling God's help in the past (61:4–5). The psalmist recalled God's past favors and used this as a basis for pleading for assistance in the present. He used several metaphors or images to convey God's protection: refuge, tent, shelter of God's wings. At verse 5 the mood of the psalm changes to bright assurance.

A prayer for the king (61:6–7). The congregation or chorus would offer this prayer for the king, who was God's representative. Their petition for his long life is also a prayer that his dynasty might endure. This would assure the nation of stability under God's protection. The king is to be watched over by two guardian angels: steadfast love and faithfulness (v. 7).

The psalmist's promise (61:8). The psalmist's response was one of praise and keeping his promises (vows) to God. Gratitude to God is always a proper response for God's people.

- ■ *The congregation offered a petition for the*
- ■ *king's long life and reign. The king was to be*
- ■ *watched over by the two guardian angels of*
- ■ *steadfast love and faithfulness. Confident of*
- ■ *God's blessing, the psalmist responded with*
- ■ *praise and gratitude.*

GUIDING QUESTION
The psalmist used several metaphors to describe God's protection. What are they and what is the significance of each?

Background: There are no specific details that point to a definite period for this psalm. The circumstances of distress make Absalom's revolt a possible setting (2 Sam. 15–18).

PSALM 62: GOD ALONE

- - - -

Theme: God is a sure refuge in times of trouble.

Reader insights: A song of trust

PSALM SUMMARY
Trust in God (62:1–2, 5–7). The psalmist waited in silence on the Lord. In the silence, the psalmist had a more accurate insight. He found God to be his salvation . . . rock . . . fortress. He looked to God to deliver him and defend his honor (v. 7).

The psalmist's enemies (62:3–4). The psalmist's enemies were out to bring him down. They kept hitting him with unrelenting pressure. They were like men trying to shatter an already tottering stone wall (v. 3). His enemies were two-faced. With their mouths they praised him, but inwardly they cursed him (v. 4).

The psalmist's advice (62:8–12). The psalmist counseled his contemporaries to trust in God at all times. They were not to put their trust in extortion, robbery, or riches (v. 10).

The psalmist learned from experience to trust God's power and love (vv. 11–12). God would punish the wicked and reward the righteous. Such trust is the way to peace.

- *In his hour of need, the psalmist silently*
- *waited on the Lord. He viewed God as his*
- *salvation, rock, and fortress. God alone was*
- *his trust.*
- *The psalmist counseled his contemporaries*
- *to trust in God at all times. Experience had*
- *taught him to trust God's power and love, not*
- *extortion, stolen goods, or riches.*

Lessons in living: When trouble strikes, where do you look for your security? Some people look to their financial resources or their friends. God alone is the Christian's security. If we wait on Him, He will see us through any difficult circumstances.

GUIDING QUESTION
What are some false gods that people trust today?

Background: This is an early psalm that likely predates the Exile. (Note the mention of the king in v. 11.) David wrote this psalm while in the wilderness, and it could be viewed as linked with Psalms 61 and 62.

PSALM 63: YOU ARE MY GOD

Theme: The longing of an exile for God

Reader insights: A song of trust

PSALM SUMMARY

The psalmist's faith in God (63:1–8). He longed for God with his "soul" and "body"—his whole being (v. 1). This has its roots in the intimate communion he enjoyed in the sanctuary (v. 2). In worship the psalmist had experienced God's presence, power, and glory (v. 2). Now, in the wilderness, he felt a keen sense of deprivation.

The psalmist concluded that God's steadfast love is more precious than life, which is mere biological existence (v. 3). In verse 4 the psalmist practiced both praise and prayer. Having the hands lifted up was the Jewish position of prayer, not kneeling with bowed head.

Experiencing life in the presence of God is like enjoying a rich banquet (v. 5). The psalmist felt as though he were feasting on God. The quiet hours of the night became a time for meditation and reflection on the greatness and protection of God (vv. 6–7).

"Not to receive honorable burial was a thought which filled the Oriental with horror" (A. Cohen, ed., *The Psalms* [New York: Soncino Press, 1974], 198).

The fate of the psalmist's enemies (63:9–11). The psalmist's enemies were God's enemies and the king's enemies as well. They were "liars" (v. 11) and had persecuted him without cause. They would go down to death and be given to the sword; they would not be buried (vv. 9–10). Their corpses would "become food for jackals." The king would rejoice at their defeat, and he would rejoice in the Lord (v. 11).

- *The psalmist longed for God with his whole*
- *being. He concluded that God's steadfast love*
- *is more precious than life itself. He was com-*
- *pletely dependent on God. The psalmist's*
- *enemies, who had persecuted him, would be*
- *defeated. They would not die an honorable*
- *death.*

GUIDING QUESTION

How did the psalmist describe his longing for God?

Background: The psalmist was being persecuted by enemies and sought refuge with God. The language resembles earlier psalms that tell of Saul's persecution of David.

PSALM 64: "NOBODY KNOWS"

Theme: Divine judgment of the wicked

Reader insights: This psalm is a personal lament against the psalmist's slanderous enemies.

PSALM SUMMARY

The psalmist's petition (64:1–6). His enemy was secretive and scheming (vv. 1–2). Note the vivid metaphors the psalmist used to describe them in verse 3 (RSV): They "whet their tongues like swords." They "aim bitter words like arrows." Sharp and stinging speech was shot from ambush by cowardly enemies (v. 4).

The psalmist's enemies never suspected that their identity would be known. They had been so cunning and secretive that they were sure they could do evil and go undetected (v. 6). The psalmist asked God for protection.

God grants the psalmist's request (64:7–10). The psalmist was confident that God would judge his enemies. In fact, he was so confident that he spoke of it as though it were already an accomplished fact. Their destruction would come suddenly. The result is that "the righteous rejoice" (v. 10) and "all mankind will fear" the Lord (v. 9). Evil does not triumph for long.

- *The psalmist's enemies were scheming*
- *against him. He petitioned God for protec-*
- *tion and security. The psalmist was confident*
- *that God would judge his enemies and spoke*
- *as though it were an accomplished fact.*

GUIDING QUESTION
What were the psalmist's enemies doing to him?

PSALM 65:
GOD'S BOUNTY

Theme: Praise to God for His provision and the prospect of an abundant harvest

Reader insights: A Zion song. Praise is due God for His spiritual blessing (forgiveness) and for His bountiful provision of the good earth.

Background: This Davidic hymn was sung in the spring, celebrating the rains that make fertile land productive.

PSALM SUMMARY

Praise in the Temple (65:1–4). The courtyards of God's holy Temple ring with hymns and prayers of praise. He has forgiven His people's sins (v. 3). They enjoy His presence in worship (v. 4).

God's mighty acts (65:5–8). God delivers and saves His people (v. 5). Since the beginning, He has been the God of their salvation. By His creative power He raises the mountains and calms the "roaring . . . seas . . . waves . . . turmoil" (vv. 6–7). Morning and evening are sent by God and "shout for joy" (v. 8, NRSV).

God's mighty provision (65:9–13). God waters the earth. "You care for the land and water it" (v. 9). This vital provision was especially important for those living in arid Israel. The failure of winter rains would mean famine. Soft rainfall filled the furrows and made the fertile soil productive.

With a poet's eye, the psalmist described the rain-washed wilderness dripping with freshness (v. 12). The green meadows were "clothed" with white flocks, and the fertile valleys wore a waving mantle of grain. Small wonder all nature would "shout for joy and sing" (v. 13).

God chooses people, forgives their sins, and satisfies them with the bounty of the good earth. This causes the psalmist to praise God!

- *God waters the earth. It is a resource without*
- *which life cannot exist in the deserts of*
- *Israel. The psalmist praised God for His*
- *bountiful provisions.*

GUIDING QUESTION

In what ways does God bless His people through His creation?

PSALM 66: GRATITUDE, BOTH CORPORATE AND PERSONAL

Background: It is difficult to determine the psalm's occasion with any degree of certainty. It does have some common features of other psalms that celebrate God's saving Judah from Assyria (2 Kings 19).

Theme: Praise for deliverance from a national crisis

Reader insights: A hymn of testimony. This is a joyful hymn of praise on behalf of the nation and the psalmist.

PSALM SUMMARY

The nation's praise of God (66:1–12). This psalm begins with the same words as Psalm 100. In the first stanza all people are invited to praise God: "All the earth bows down to you" (v. 4). The second stanza describes God's mighty deliverance from slavery through the Exodus. The psalmist's description of oppression is vivid. It is like the hot fire that refines silver (v. 10). The people feel as though they are trapped in a net with no way of escape (v. 11). Others overwhelm them, and they go "through fire and water" (v. 12). Yet God delivers His people. The people are brought to a "place of abundance." This abundance is an antithesis to the deprivations they had experienced, and just as distinct.

The psalmist's praise of God (66:13–20). This section is a song of thanksgiving. The psalmist paid his vows in gratitude for God's deliverance when he was in trouble (vv. 13–14). Out of gratitude he brought many offerings: rams, bulls, and goats (v. 15).

- ■ *The psalmist paid his vows in gratitude for*
- ■ *God's deliverance when he was in trouble.*
- ■ *This passage is an outpouring of gratitude*
- ■ *for God's deliverance.*

GUIDING QUESTION

What kinds of oppression did God's people endure that required God's deliverance?

PSALM 67: A HYMN AT HARVEST

- - - -

Theme: Universal praise for God

Reader insights: A blessing psalm

PSALM SUMMARY

God blesses Israel (67:1–5). This harvest hymn begins with the ancient blessing of Aaron (Num. 6:24–26). God's face shining upon us is a poetic way of speaking about divine favor. But He also judges (rules fairly) and guides the other nations of the earth (vv. 4–5).

God as Deliverer

To deliver is to rescue from danger. God as deliverer of His people is one of the great themes of the Old Testament. In Scripture God gives deliverance (Pss. 18:50; 32:7; 44:4), often through a human agent. In the Old Testament, deliverance most often refers to victory in battle (Judg. 15:18; 2 Kings 5:1; 13:17; 1 Chron. 11:14; 2 Chron. 12:7). Joseph was God's agent to deliver His people from famine (Gen. 45:7). The Old Testament consistently emphasizes God as the giver of deliverance rather than the human agent. Thus Mordecai warned Esther that if she failed to act out her role as deliverer, God would provide another way (Esth. 4:14).

Background: Some interpreters connect this psalm with Psalm 65 as a hymn of thanksgiving for an abundant harvest that followed soon after the victory over Assyria.

31

God blesses the nations (67:4–7). God provides the bountiful harvest. He blesses us, and all people everywhere should revere and worship the Lord (vv. 6–7). This psalm has a strong missionary thrust. Gratitude to God is a motive for making God's way known beyond Israel.

■ *It is God who provides the harvest. The*
■ *psalmist emphasized that all people every-*
■ *where should revere and worship the Lord.*
■ *We see in this section the psalm's strong mis-*
■ *sionary thrust.*

GUIDING QUESTION

What does it mean for God's face to shine upon His people?

Lessons in living: In keeping with the missionary thrust of this psalm, resolve to experience the fullness of God's grace by telling others about the good news of Jesus Christ.

PSALM 68: GOD IS KING

Theme: The triumphant march of God throughout the history of Israel

Reader insights: A victory song

PSALM SUMMARY

An invocation (68:1–3). These words were sung at the beginning of the processional. The ark of the covenant, representing God's presence, led the worshipers ("may God arise"). God's enemies flee before Him, but the righteous are joyful.

God's actions in history (68:4–18). God is the ideal King who reverses the fortunes of those who are oppressed. Here we have a rehearsal of God's historic actions on behalf of His people in the

Background: This psalm became a battle song of the Protestant Reformation. It is a collection of short hymns used in the dramatic worship of Israel, celebrating God as King. Its roots are found in the Song of Deborah (Judg. 5).

Exodus (vv. 7–10). The defeat of Sisera is a typical example of the victories God gave Israel (vv. 11–14). God chose Mount Zion for His abode. He came there from Mount Sinai, leading captives and receiving gifts. The imagery is that of a warrior-king in triumphal procession.

Paul applies this scene to the victorious Christ after His resurrection (v. 18; see Eph. 4:8).

God, our Savior (68:19–23). God is the source of our salvation (v. 19). In verse 23 the psalmist speaks in no uncertain terms of vengeance. Notice the graphic imagery: "That you may plunge your feet in the blood of your foes, while the tongues of your dogs have their share."

The "hairy crowns" (v. 21) refer to a warrior's oath not to cut his hair until he has defeated his enemy in battle.

Worship processional (68:24–27). A great procession of worshipers went up to the sanctuary to worship. They were led by singers who were followed by young women, princes, and musicians.

"The beast among the reeds" (v. 30) refers to the crocodiles and hippopotami that live in the marshes along the Nile River.

God's majesty and power (68:28–35). Various nations are told to acknowledge God's might and majesty. Egypt is one nation singled out. Ethiopia is asked to recognize the God of Israel who strikes awe in those who worship Him (vv. 31, 35). All nations are invited to sing His praise.

■ *Various nations are told to acknowledge*
■ *God's might and majesty, and all nations are*
■ *invited to sing His praise.*

GUIDING QUESTIONS

What is this psalm's setting? Why has it been so celebrated?

PSALM 69: REPROACH FOR SERVING GOD

Theme: Suffering of the righteous believer at the hands of the godless

Reader insights: An individual lament

PSALM SUMMARY

The psalmist's predicament (69:1–12). The psalmist cried out for God to save him (v. 1), describing his plight as that of a man caught in a flood or quicksand (vv. 2–5). He grew weary waiting for divine deliverance.

The psalmist's enemies were many and fierce. They hated him without cause and were out to destroy him (v. 4). He did not claim to be sinless (v. 5). But he had been reproached because of his faith (vv. 7, 9). His own brothers did not recognize him (v. 8). Even the town drunks made fun of him (v. 12).

The psalmist's prayer (69:13–29). He asked for God's help and rescue lest "the depths swallow me up" (v. 15). After all, heaven knew what he was suffering (v. 19). The psalmist received no sympathy or understanding—only scorn and reproach (vv. 20–21). The psalmist (vv. 22–29) cursed his enemies eloquently. He asked that they might go blind and be afflicted with palsy. He prayed that the divine anger might be vented on those who hated both him and God. Asking the ultimate punishment, he wanted his foes "blotted out of the book of the life" (v. 28).

The psalmist's praise (69:30–36). He promised to give thanks to the Lord (v. 30). Those who are oppressed will see how the Lord delivers him and "be glad" (v. 32). Finally, the psalmist called on heaven and earth to praise the Lord (v. 34). God would save Zion and rebuild the cities of Judah (v. 35).

- *The psalmist's enemies were out to destroy*
- *him, and he was growing weary of waiting*
- *for God's help.*
- *He asked that his enemies receive the ulti-*
- *mate punishment. He promised to give*
- *thanks to the Lord, and called on heaven and*
- *earth to praise the Lord.*

GUIDING QUESTION

Why is this psalm quoted so often in the New Testament?

PSALM 70: A TESTIMONY TO ANSWERED PRAYER

Theme: Thanksgiving for deliverance from trouble

Reader insights: An individual lament

Background: These verses were apparently detached from Psalm 40 to form a separate psalm for use in Temple liturgy.

PSALM SUMMARY

A cry for help (70:1–3). Although we do not know the specifics of the psalmist's situation, we can see that he is in serious trouble. He spoke to God in a desperate tone.

Praise for God (70:4–5). The psalmist's cries for help turned into praise for God.

He felt his own weakness but was equally aware of God's power. Therefore, he could trust God to take care of him.

■ *The psalmist praised God and then placed*
■ *his trust in Him.*

GUIDING QUESTION

What is the relationship of this psalm to Psalm 40?

PSALM 71: AN AGED MAN'S PRAYER

Theme: Assurance of God's protection in old age

Reader insights: An individual lament

Background: The petitioner of this prayer was an elderly man in imminent danger of death, being pursued and accused by his enemies. The psalm is similar to and quotes from others (22; 31; 35; 40; 57).

PSALM SUMMARY

The old man's doubt (71:1–21). The psalmist trusted the Lord despite his distress. He considered God his fortress, refuge, and rock. He made several pleas to God that indicated his state of desperation. He had trusted the Lord from his youth (v. 5) and had served him all his life (v. 6*b*). The elderly psalmist's enemies thought that God had forsaken him and that they could take advantage of him with impunity (vv. 11–12).

In verses 9 and 18*a* we have the poignant prayer of the elderly, that God will not forsake the psalmist in his old age. He has been a faithful member of the covenant community. If spared, he promised to proclaim God's might to subsequent generations (v. 18*b*). The psalmist recalled God's providential care in times past (v. 20). He now trusted the Lord to spare him and revive him again (vv. 20*b*–21).

The old man's praise (71:22–24). The greatness of God almost overwhelmed the psalmist (v. 19).

This led him to praise the Lord with the harp and lyre, with his lips and tongue. His enemies had been routed (v. *24b*). In verse 22 he addressed God as the "Holy One of Israel."

- *The petitioner of this prayer was an elderly*
- *man in imminent danger of death, being pur-*
- *sued and accused by his enemies. Over-*
- *whelmed by God's greatness, the psalmist*
- *praised God with song and music.*

Lessons in living: Each stage of life presents unique challenges and advantages. We may be encouraged that God stays with us through each stage. No matter our age, we can always live in such a way as to bring glory to God.

GUIDING QUESTION

What assurances did the old man embrace?

PSALM 72: PRAYER FOR THE KING

Theme: A prayer for blessing for the chosen king

Reader insights: A coronation song. This prayer may have been written for Solomon. It looks beyond to a greater King—Jesus Christ.

Background: The prayer was probably written by someone in the court on behalf of the king. It is a royal psalm and may have been used in conjunction with coronations, perhaps King Solomon's.

PSALM SUMMARY

Righteous rule (72:1–4). The psalmist prayed that the king, the royal son, might rule with God's justice and righteousness (vv. 1–2). He also asked for prosperity, a sign of divine favor (v. 3), and for the king to defend the poor and crush their oppressors (v. 4).

Long life (72:5–7). The psalmist asked that the king might "endure as long as the sun." This does not imply his immortality. Rather, it is more a prayer for the perpetuation of his dynasty and for his rule to be as welcome and prosperous as the life-giving spring showers. After the first mowing, spring rains produce an even more abundant crop.

In verse 7, the Hebrew word, *shalom*, translated "prosperity" is also translated "peace."

Dominion from sea to sea (72:8–17). The psalmist prayed that the king's rule might extend "from sea to sea" (from the Mediterranean to the Persian Gulf). "The River" was probably the Euphrates, and Tarshish was Spain. Sheba was in Arabia, and Seba was in Ethiopia (Africa). These were the limits of the world known to the psalmist.

He also prayed that the king's enemies would "lick the dust" (v. 9); that is, bow before him paying homage. The king is to be the champion of the powerless (vv. 12–14). The psalmist hoped that the king, like Abraham, would be the channel of divine blessings to "all nations" (v. 17*b*).

Signs of God's favor on the king's rule will include long life, fruitful harvests, a growing population, and fame that lasts "as long as the sun" (v. 17*a*).

Lessons in living: While this psalm may have been written for Solomon, an Old Testament king, one day Christ will return to establish His kingdom on the earth. Today He is establishing His kingdom in the hearts of believers everywhere.

■ *The psalmist asked that the king might be*
■ *prosperous and that his enemies might pay*
■ *him homage.*

CONCLUSION TO BOOK II (72:18–20)

Here we have a doxology that marks the end of the second division of the Psalter. Verse 20 is an editorial footnote indicating that there are no further psalms of David.

GUIDING QUESTION

Scholars believe this is a messianic psalm. Why?

Theme: The problem of evil

Reader insights: A wisdom song

PSALM SUMMARY

The theme stated (73:1–3). Mankind has always been troubled by the problem of why God permits evil. Old Testament people had an even more acute problem. They had no clear revelation of life after death. They believed the righteous were blessed by God and the wicked were punished here on earth. When they saw evidence to the contrary, they didn't know how to handle it. This nearly caused the psalmist to lose his faith!

Background: The psalmist was deeply troubled by the sight of wicked people triumphing and flourishing. Their defiance of God brought no judgment, whereas the righteous suffered. His faith was being sorely tested.

The darkness of doubt (73:4–14). The psalmist was emphatic. Look at the prosperous wicked! They are proud, violent oppressors. Yet they never appear to suffer pain. They are in perfect health (v. 4) and never in trouble. They are indulgent gluttons (v. 7) while others go hungry. They are irreverent scoffers who believe God is unaware of their meanness (v. 11). Ironically, they are well thought of in the community (v. 10). Everything they touch turns to gold (v. 12).

This is one of the major themes of the Book of Job.

He now contemplated the situation. What good does it do the psalmist to live a clean life? All he gets for it is trouble (vv. 13–14). These circumstances are enough to try anyone's faith.

The brightness of faith affirmed (73:15–28). The psalmist was wearied by trying to figure out the answer to his question (v. 16). The turning point came when he went to worship (v. 17). Suddenly he realized that the wicked were not as secure as they seemed. One false step, and they will fall to ruin (v. 18). Their prosperity—indeed, their lives—is temporary. They can lose it all in a flash (v. 19). They are as insubstantial as a dream that vanishes when a person wakes up (v. 20).

The psalmist repented of his bitterness and lack of faith (vv. 21–22). He realized that he was in fellowship with God, who upheld him, guided him, and would receive him "into glory" (vv. 23–24).

While the psalmist didn't get specific answers to why the wicked prosper and the righteous suffer, he found fulfillment in being in the presence of God. The reward of faith and the ultimate answer of prayer is "to be near God" (v. 28). Here we have a contrast between the passing pleasures of the sinner and the enduring peace of those who are friends of God.

- *The problem of evil has always plagued us.*
- *The psalmist struggled with why God per-*
- *mits it. The wicked prosper. They are proud*
- *and violent oppressors of the righteous. Yet*
- *they never appear to suffer pain. It was a*
- *severe test of the psalmist's faith. The turning*
- *point came when the psalmist went to wor-*
- *ship. He repented of his lack of faith and bit-*
- *terness. Although he did not get an answer to*
- *the problem of evil or the prosperity of the*
- *wicked, he did get fulfillment from being in*
- *the presence of God.*

GUIDING QUESTION

What helped the psalmist come to terms with his questions about why the wicked prosper and the righteous suffer?

PSALM 74: GOD'S HOUSE IN RUINS

- - - -

Theme: A prayer for redemption

Reader insights: A community lament

PSALM SUMMARY

The people's lament (74:1–3). The people felt rejected and punished due to God's anger (v. 1). Pathetically, they asked God to remember them and Mount Zion, where once He dwelled on earth (v. 2). His sanctuary had been completely destroyed by the enemy (v. 3).

Destruction (74:4–8). God's enemies (and Israel's) shouted ("roared") with delight at their destructive power, putting up their own banners in His holy place (v. 4). The enemy's shouts replaced Israel's praise in the Temple. Then they hacked the Temple to pieces and set it on fire (vv. 5–7). They burned every worship assembly place in Israel (v. 8).

No prophet in the land (74:9–11). Even worse than the destruction of their capital and Temple was the silence of God. The voice of the prophets was no longer heard. There was no word from the Lord. How long would such unbearable conditions continue (v. 10)?

God is still king (74:12–17). God alone can save His people (v. 12). The psalmist then cited the

Background: Here we have a congregation's lament at the destruction of the Temple. The historical reference is most likely Nebuchadnezzar's conquest of Jerusalem in 586 B.C. (2 Kings 25).

41

mighty acts of God in the past: creation and deliverance from Egypt.

A prayer for remembrance and redemption (74:18–23). The psalmist prayed that God's people, helpless as doves, would not be given to the wild beasts (v. 19). He asked God to "have regard for your covenant" (v. 20) and to "rise up" and remember His people (vv. 22–23).

Hosea compared God's people to doves (Hos. 7:11; 11:11).

GUIDING QUESTION

What was the likely occasion for this psalm?

Background: This psalm was a liturgy used in worship at the Temple in Jerusalem. The people chanted verse 1.

PSALM 75: GOD, THE DIVINE JUDGE

Theme: The judgment of God

Reader insights: An oracle psalm

PSALM SUMMARY

God's acts (75:1–3). The congregation will recount the "wonderful deeds" of the Almighty on their behalf. God's strength and His sovereignty are seen in His deeds on behalf of Israel.

God's message (75:4–8). God warned against pride and boasting. The psalmist depicted divine judgment here as a bitter cup of wine (v. 8). It must be drained "down to its very dregs" as punishment for evildoing. All people's lives are in the hand of Providence: "He brings one down, he exalts another" (v. 7).

"Do not lift up your horns" (v. 5). This is a warning to the wicked. The "horn" was a symbol of animal strength. The wicked were arrogant people who were proud of their power.

In praise of God (75:9–10). A soloist or chanter here praised God for humiliating the wicked and exalting the righteous. God alone can judge, and His judgment is often surprising!

- *God must judge evildoing. The psalmist*
- *praised God for humiliating the wicked and*
- *exalting the righteous.*

GUIDING QUESTION

What two wrongs does this psalm address?

PSALM 76: WHEN WRATH TURNS TO PRAISE

Theme: Defeat of Israel's enemies and the glorification of God

Reader insights: A hymn

PSALM SUMMARY

God in Salem (76:1–6). God established His residence in Jerusalem. There God destroyed the enemies' weapons of war. He rendered helpless both soldiers and war horses.

God in judgment (76:7–12). God is terrible in His wrath (v. 7). No person or thing can withstand His anger. He comes from heaven in judgment, and the earth is gripped by fear (v. 8). But note that He exercises judgment on behalf of the poor and the oppressed (v. 9).

God's wrath against humankind brings praise (v. 10). Human wrath only adds to God's glory, for He overrules human schemes (Rom. 9:17). God is not frustrated by evil but defeats it. The people are told to pay their vows and bring their gifts in gratitude and praise toward God (v. 11).

Background: Like Psalms 46 and 48, this psalm celebrates God's presence on Mount Zion. It is also a celebration of divine deliverance and victory over Israel's enemies. The historical reference may be to King Hezekiah's victory over Sennacherib in 701 B.C. (2 Kings 18–19). However, it applies to God-given victory at any time.

Salem is another name for the city of peace. The related word, *shalom*, means peace in Hebrew.

■ *God's judgment is certain. When He comes to*
■ *judge, the earth is gripped by fear, for no one*
■ *can withstand God's wrath.*

GUIDING QUESTION

What two responses does God's wrath bring from people?

Background: In the midst of hard times, the psalmist calls for historical perspective.

PSALM 77: THE LONG VIEW OF FAITH

Theme: Hope in the midst of troubled times

Reader insights: Although this lament is voiced by an individual, it relates to the whole nation.

PSALM SUMMARY

Their present trouble (77:1–10). The psalmist cried aloud to God in prayer but felt that he was not being heard. Day and night he sought relief (v. 2). He stayed awake at night thinking and reflecting. God had been gracious to Israel in the past (v. 5). Would He now spurn her forever (v. 7)?

Their future hope is based on God's previous grace (77:11–20). After reflecting on God's mighty deeds of the past (vv. 11–12), the psalmist sang praises of his God. God is unique, the only true God. He is Creator and Sustainer. He led His people through the Red Sea.

- *Although the psalmist cried aloud to God in*
- *prayer, he felt that he was not heard. He*
- *began to question God. He wondered if*
- *indeed God had withdrawn from the nation.*
- *For God's people, future hope was based on*
- *God's previous grace. In this passage the*
- *psalmist spoke of three mighty acts of God:*
- *creation, the thunderstorm, and the Israel-*
- *ites' great Exodus from Egypt.*

GUIDING QUESTION

What was the psalmist's basis for hope?

PSALM 78: LESSONS FROM HISTORY

Theme: The theme of this psalm is the repeated disobedience of God's people in spite of all His mighty acts on their behalf.

Reader insights: A wisdom psalm

PSALM SUMMARY

Lest we forget (78:1–66). The psalmist explored the riddle of rebellion. He took on the role of teacher, drawing lessons from three great events in Israel's history: the Exodus from Egypt, the wilderness wanderings, and the conquest of Canaan. Once in the Promised Land, the people adopted the idolatry of the Canaanites. God's response was to forsake His dwelling place at Shiloh and allow the ark of the covenant to fall into the hands of the foe. The psalmist's purpose was that his readers might learn from the past

Background: The psalmist surveyed Israel's history from the bondage in Egypt to King David's reign. His reference toward the end of the psalm to the Temple as still in existence strongly suggests that he composed this psalm before the Babylonian captivity.

mistakes of their ancestors. The psalm may well have been read at observances of Passover.

God's choice (78:67–72). In His grace God chose the tribe of Judah for His people (v. 68). He chose Mount Zion as the site of His presence, in the Temple (v. 69). He chose the shepherd boy, David, to become the shepherd of His people (v. 70).

- *God was gracious to His people in spite of*
- *their rebellion and ingratitude.*

GUIDING QUESTION
What applications from this psalm might we make today?

PSALM 79: NATIONAL CALAMITY

Background: The setting of this psalm appears almost certainly to be the Babylonian invasion of Judah in 587 B.C. Although Jerusalem was considered to be impregnable, the Babylonians defiled the Temple and destroyed Jerusalem. (See Ps. 74, which is similar.) The destruction of their Holy City and the deportation of the Jews into Exile has been called "The Old Testament Passion Story."

Theme: Lament over the destruction of Jerusalem and the deportation of her people

Reader insights: This psalm is a national lament.

PSALM SUMMARY
Catastrophe! (79:1–7). The psalmist began by describing the basis of his lament. His psalm must have been composed very soon after the destruction of the city. The memory seems fresh in his mind. He simply cannot believe what has happened! Jerusalem was thought to enjoy divine protection. The psalmist prayed that God would turn His anger on the kingdoms who "devoured Jacob and destroyed his homeland" (v. 7).

Fixing blame (79:8–9). First, the psalmist lashed out against Judah's destructive enemies. Next he acknowledged that one reason for the calamity was "the sins of the fathers." Finally, he came to acknowledge personal responsibility: "Deliver us and forgive our sins for your name's sake."

"Help us, O God" (79:10–13). The psalmist cried for help for two reasons: (1) the great need of God's people and (2) the honor of God's name.

■ *The psalmist described the basis of his*
■ *lament. The heathen had ravaged the Temple*
■ *and left Jerusalem in ruins. He prayed that*
■ *God would turn His anger on those nations*
■ *who had perpetrated these atrocities on*
■ *Israel.*

GUIDING QUESTION
In spite of the difficulties the psalmist endured, his closing remarks were praise to God. What motivated him to do so in the midst of such distress?

PSALM 80: SHEPHERD OF ISRAEL

Theme: The restoration of the nation

Reader insights: This is a psalm of community lament.

Background: We cannot be sure of this psalm's historical setting. One suggestion is that it was written at the fall of the city of Samaria to the Assyrians in 721 B.C.

PSALM SUMMARY
Shepherd of Israel (80:1–3). The psalm opens by addressing God as "Shepherd of Israel"—as one who is enthroned between the cherubim. The

psalmist called on God to let His face shine on His people so they might be saved. He repeated this petition three times throughout the psalm.

Lord God Almighty (80:4–7). Next the psalmist addressed God as Lord God Almighty. There is some irony in his using this title and then asking God why He had made His people drink their tears by the bowlful (v. 5).

To say that God is enthroned above the cherubim means He inhabits the Holy of Holies. Cherubs were angelic figures atop the ark of the covenant (1 Kings 6:23–28). Between them was the mercy seat where God's presence was localized.

"A vine out of Egypt" (80:8–19). The psalmist depicted Israel as a young vine which God took from Egypt and transplanted in Canaan. Unless a vine fulfills its purpose of bearing grapes, it is worthless. Jesus taught that unless believers abide in Him, they "can do nothing" (John 15:5).

The transplanted vine, Israel, was very prosperous. It took root and filled the land (v. 9). Its branches reached from the sea to the Euphrates River. That was the extent of David and Solomon's kingdom (vv. 10–11).

But something happened. Because of the people's unfaithfulness, God broke down the protective wall surrounding Israel. Thieves could pluck the fruit, and wild boars could get in and root up the vine (vv. 12–13). These verses constitute a vivid metaphor of what was happening. The vine was being destroyed (v. 16).

The psalmist prayed for God's favor and blessing on the king and the people (v. 17). He promised that they would continue to worship and serve the Lord. "We will not turn away from you" is a vow of fidelity. The absence of God was temporary. The psalmist then repeated his petition that God's face would shine on His people so they might be saved.

- *God is Israel's Shepherd, which speaks of His*
- *care of them and their dependence upon Him.*
- *The psalmist asked God to save His people*
- *and restore them. God's wrath had caused*
- *His people to experience the scorn of their*
- *enemies and neighbors. The psalmist*
- *depicted Israel as a young vine which God*
- *took from Egypt and transplanted in*
- *Canaan. Because of Israel's unfaithfulness,*
- *God took away His protection. The psalmist*
- *prayed for God's favor and blessing on the*
- *king and the people.*

GUIDING QUESTION

What two metaphors did the psalmist use to describe God's relationship with Israel?

PSALM 81: REMEMBRANCE AND WARNING

Theme: Thanksgiving to God for abundant harvests

Reader insights: Call to praise and prophetic warning

PSALM SUMMARY

The thanksgiving hymn (81:1–5b). The psalm begins with a colorful call to praise. It includes singing, shouting, and instrumental music. The trumpet (v. 3) was the *shofar* or ram's horn.

A prophetic sermon (81:5c–16). A message is given to Israel by a prophet who speaks for God. He rehearses the highlights of Hebrew history.

Background: There are three possible occasions for this psalm: (1) the Feast of Tabernacles, which took place in autumn, (2) the Jewish New Year, and (3) Passover.

God had delivered them from burdensome toil and bondage in Egypt (vv. 6–7). God had answered them in the thunder from Mount Sinai (v. 7; see Exod. 19:19). God had tested them at the waters of Meribah in the wilderness (Exod. 17:1–7).

Next, the prophet reminded his listeners of the Law of God. They were not to serve any "foreign god" (v. 9 NIV; see Exod. 20:3). And they were always to remember: "I am the LORD your God" (v. 10; see Exod. 20:1–2). The children of Israel owed God their full allegiance for delivering them from slavery in Egypt. In a similar way, Christians owe their first loyalty to God through Jesus Christ for their deliverance from bondage to sin.

The Israelites were disobedient, choosing to go their own headstrong way (vv. 11–12). Thus, God gave them their way and left them to their own devices (see Rom. 1:24–32 for a parallel passage). Still, God pleaded for them to obey Him and be blessed (vv. 13–16).

Even in the midst of their celebration, the people needed to hear this warning. They needed to remember the source of their prosperity and blessings and be grateful. People are in a dangerous spiritual state when they have no desire for God (v. 11).

- *The psalm begins with a call to praise and*
- *points to the basic observances of the festival.*
- *The psalmist rehearsed the highlights of*
- *Hebrew history, warning his listeners they*
- *were not to serve any "foreign god."*

GUIDING QUESTIONS
What is the psalmist's lesson for his readers? What lessons might we gain from the message of this psalm?

PSALM 82: JUDGE OF HEAVEN AND EARTH

- - - -

Theme: A call for God's judgment for those administering injustice and partiality

Reader insights: An oracle psalm

PSALM SUMMARY

The heavenly court (82:1–4). The psalmist imagined the heathen gods assembled before the throne of God (v. 1), where God accused them of being unjust and of showing partiality to the wicked (v. 2). They had not dealt fairly with the weak, the destitute, and those who were oppressed (vv. 3–4). Injustice on earth is a result of serving false gods who do not have the high ethical standards of the true God (the Ten Commandments).

Background: God called Israel's administrators of justice to account for failing to discharge their office properly. The circumstances are the same in Psalm 83.

The judgment of the loving God (82:5–8). Pagan gods are not enlightened or intelligent (v. 5). Neither are they immortal; they die with the people who serve them (vv. 6–7). Who in the world today worships Zeus, Venus, or Thor? No nation ever rises above the ethical level of its gods, its highest loyalty. Pagans and false gods alike die. The worshipers in verse 8 acknowledged God as the real Judge of the earth, to whom all nations belong.

■ *The psalmist imagined the heathen gods*
■ *assembled before the throne of God, where*
■ *God accused them of injustice and partial-*
■ *ity. Pagan gods lack understanding and*
■ *intelligence. They die with their culture.*
■ *There is only one living God who deserves*
■ *our worship.*

GUIDING QUESTION

According to this psalm, what is the source of injustice on the earth?

PSALM 83: ENEMIES OF GOD

Background: It appears that we have an historical collection of Israel's enemies listed here. Not all of these foes existed at the same time. However, the reference to Assyria in verse 8 would date the psalm around the last half of the eighth century B.C. The Assyrian Empire came to prominence under the leadership of King Tiglath-pileser III.

Theme: A national prayer for God's help

Reader insights: A national lament, in which the people curse their oppressors

PSALM SUMMARY

A national crisis (83:1–8). The psalmist pleaded for God's attention to Israel's plight (v. 1). Their enemies, and His, had formed a deadly conspiracy. They had plotted to wipe out the nation (vv. 4–5).

A curse on their enemies (83:9–18). The psalmist asked God to do to His enemies what had been done to past enemies. Then he gave concrete examples of God's past deliverance. He prayed for natural disasters to come to God's enemies so people would recognize God and seek Him.

- The psalmist asked God to deliver the nation
- and give examples of God's past deliverance.
- The psalmist then put a curse on Israel's ene-
- mies, asking that God put them to shame and
- vindicate His name.

GUIDING QUESTION

In this psalm, what is the purpose of remembering God's acts of deliverance?

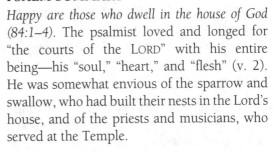

PSALM 84:
AT HOME WITH GOD

Theme: Communion with God in the sanctuary

Reader insights: A processional hymn. This psalm contains three beatitudes (vv. 4–5, 12).

PSALM SUMMARY

Happy are those who dwell in the house of God (84:1–4). The psalmist loved and longed for "the courts of the LORD" with his entire being—his "soul," "heart," and "flesh" (v. 2). He was somewhat envious of the sparrow and swallow, who had built their nests in the Lord's house, and of the priests and musicians, who served at the Temple.

Happy are the pilgrims en route to Zion (84:5–9). Not only were those who served at the Temple blessed; so were the worshipers who came as pilgrims (v. 5). Even those who passed through the Valley of Baca—a time of great sorrow—were blessed.

God's people "go from strength to strength" (v. 7). The journey does not cause them to be exhausted, for they receive help that sees them through. His presence is the source of their renewal. The psalmist recited his prayers for the king in verses 8–9.

Happy are those who trust in the Lord (84:10–12). Better to be a lowly servant in God's house than to live anywhere else. God is the psalmist's "sun"—his light and warmth. The Lord is his "shield"—his protection and providence. God gives those whose "walk is blameless" His favor, honor, and prosperity (v. 11).

Background: The psalmist was a pilgrim en route to the autumn festival (at the time of the early rains in October, v. 6). He longed for the experience of celebrative worship. He envied those who serve in the Temple full-time. The psalmist celebrated the joy of worship in the Lord's presence, not simply the beauty of Solomon's Temple.

- *The psalmist longed for the courts of the*
- *Lord with his entire being. The worshipers*
- *who came as pilgrims to the festival were*
- *blessed. They received help from the God*
- *who sees them through their journey. Blessed*
- *is the person who trusts in the Lord! God is*
- *the believer's "sun" and "shield."*

GUIDING QUESTION

Describe the pilgrims' journey to Zion. What sustained them for the long trek?

PSALM 85: "RESTORE US AGAIN"

Theme: Prayer for revival after return from exile in Babylon

Reader insights: A community lament

PSALM SUMMARY

God's favor in times past (85:1–3). The people had returned from exile. God had restored the fortunes of His people. In 538 B.C. they returned to their homeland under the kindness of Cyrus, the Persian conqueror of Babylon. The people took this as a sign of God's forgiveness and grace. The Lord had restored, forgiven, and pardoned them, withdrawing His wrath.

Lord, do it again now (85:4–7). The present status of the people was not as bright as the expectations of the prophet of the Exile (Isa. 40–66). The long-neglected land was poor, and times were hard. They were rebuilding their capital

Background: The setting of this psalm appears to be just after the return of the Jews from exile in Babylon. That would have been in the time of Zechariah and Haggai. The Exile was considered a judgment of God on the Hebrews for their idolatry and iniquity. That was the theme of the eighth-century B.C. prophets.

city and the Temple, but it lacked the glory of Solomon's day.

The people prayed that God would revive them again and restore the nation to its former greatness. The psalmist must have had in mind their spiritual health as well as their political security (v. 7).

Expectations for the future (85:8–13). This section of the psalm must have been recited by a worship leader, a priest, or prophet. It gave assurance of God's future grace toward His people: "He promises peace to his people" (v. 8). God and His creation were in harmony.

The Temple of Zerubbabel was completed in 516 B.C. and enhanced by King Herod in Jesus' generation. But the ultimate realization of God's glory in the midst of His people came with the incarnation of God in Christ (John 1:14).

■ *God had restored the fortunes of His people.*
■ *He had withdrawn His wrath and allowed*
■ *them to return from exile to their homeland.*
■ *The long-neglected land was poor, and times*
■ *were hard. The people would need God's help*
■ *to revive them again and restore the nation to*
■ *its former greatness. This passage is an*
■ *assurance of God's future grace toward His*
■ *people: "He promises peace to his people."*

GUIDING QUESTION
What did God promise to His people?

PSALM 86: "YOU ARE MY GOD"

Theme: A cry for help in time of trouble

Reader insights: An individual lament. We have an unusual structure in this psalm. It begins with a lament or plea for help, proceeds to thanksgiving, and then returns to lament.

Background: No particular circumstance can be identified as the occasion of this psalm. It appears to be a meditation to be used by a person in time of trouble.

PSALM SUMMARY

A prayer for deliverance (86:1–7). The psalmist saw himself as being poor and in need of divine aid. He was godly—a man of devout faith. He described God in the lament as being good, forgiving, and loving, and he was confident that his needs could be met by the One to whom he prayed.

A note of praise (86:8–13). God is the father of all the nations who will one day acknowledge His lordship (v. 9; Isa. 66:23).The psalmist sang his praise and thanksgiving to God for His instruction, might, and "love toward me" (v. 13). In the past the Lord had delivered him from death (Sheol).

A cry for help (86:14–17). The plea for help is renewed. The psalmist was despised for his faith by "arrogant . . . ruthless men." He asked for divine favor and vindication, an often-repeated theme in the Psalter.

■ *The psalmist renewed his plea for help. He*
■ *was being persecuted by "ruthless" men. He*
■ *not only asked for God's favor, but also for*
■ *vindication.*

GUIDING QUESTION

What was the psalmist's view of God's character?

Background: The mention of Babylon suggests a date for this psalm's composition after the return from captivity.

An ancient exile wrote: "If I forget you, O Jerusalem, may my right hand forget its skill" (Ps. 137:5). Jerusalem was more than a city with a fascinating history. It was also a symbol of our hunger for God and home and immortality.

PSALM 87: "GLORIOUS THINGS ARE SAID OF YOU"

Theme: God's City of Choice

Reader insights: An oracle psalm. This psalm is an ode to the city of Zion (Jerusalem).

PSALM SUMMARY

Zion, the city of God (87:1–3). The psalm begins with a hymn of praise to Jerusalem. God established and loved it. He chose to dwell with people in this city (v. 3).

Zion, the mother of all believers (87:4–6). People in all lands who know God look to Jerusalem as their spiritual mother. Pilgrims came there to worship from Egypt (Rahab), Babylon, Philistia, and Phoenicia (Tyre). Every believer is a citizen of two cities, his own and Jerusalem. The new birth marks us as spiritual natives of Zion.

Zion, the source of all spiritual blessings (87:7). The faith in God represented by Jerusalem is the "spring" from which all blessings flow. This final verse shows praise expressed by musicians.

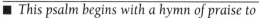

■ *This psalm begins with a hymn of praise to*
■ *Jerusalem. God established and loved it. He*
■ *chose to dwell with people in this city. People*
■ *in all lands who know God look to Jerusalem*
■ *as their spiritual mother. One day "every*
■ *knee should bow . . . and every tongue con-*
■ *fess that Jesus Christ is Lord." The faith in*
■ *God represented by Jerusalem is the "spring"*
■ *from which all blessings flow.*

"Zion"
The term *Zion* is the transliteration of the Hebrew and Greek words that originally referred to the fortified hill of pre-Israelite Jerusalem between the Kidron and Tyropean valleys. Scholars disagree as to the root meaning of the term.

GUIDING QUESTION

Why is the concept of Zion important to believers today?

PSALM 88: CRY FROM THE DEPTHS

Theme: A cry from the depths of despair

Reader insights: An individual lament

Background: This has been called "the saddest psalm." It is a cry of agony by a person who felt cut off from God. He saw no hope in this world or the next—and still he prayed.

PSALM SUMMARY

Prayer in suffering (88:1–9). The psalmist opened this psalm with an acknowledgment that God is the only source from which his deliverance can come. He prayed day and night. Yet, he was on the brink of death. In addition to his illness, he suffered the rejection of his friends (v. 8). But the greatest agony was that he felt cut off from God.

"Lord, why the darkness?" (88:10–18). The psalmists asked four rhetorical questions of God. The assumed answer to each was *no*. Instead of turning to praise or expressing hope for the future,

the psalmist continued his lamentation. He prayed early in the morning (v. 13). Still, he felt cut off and under God's judgment (v. 14). His illness dated from his youth (v. 15); perhaps he had never known what it was to be well. And yet he continued to pray.

■ *The psalmist, on the brink of death, acknowl-*
■ *edged that God was his only source of salva-*
■ *tion. He prayed to God continually. In*
■ *addition to his illness, he suffered rejection.*
■ *Searching for hope, he asked four rhetorical*
■ *questions of God, the answer to which was*
■ *no. Instead of turning to praise or expressing*
■ *hope for the future, the psalmist continued*
■ *his lamentation. The psalm is a dirge of dark*
■ *despair due to the psalmist's extended illness,*
■ *social rejection, and feeling of spiritual judg-*
■ *ment. We see the psalmist's true feelings.*

GUIDING QUESTION
The psalm ended on a dark note. What might we learn from it?

PSALM 89: GOD'S COVENANT WITH DAVID

Background: The setting of this royal psalm is a time of national crisis. It was probably used in Hebrew worship in various times of trouble, to recall God's promises. It may have been written as late as the Exile.

Theme: The overthrow of the nation by a triumphant enemy

Reader insights: A community lament. It laments that although God made an eternal covenant with the house of David, the dynasty now seemed abandoned.

PSALM SUMMARY

The preface (89:1–4). The psalmist sang of God's steadfast "love" and "faithfulness." These words appear throughout the psalm. He celebrated God's covenant promise to His servant David and to his successors (v. 4).

God's power as Creator and sustainer (89:5–18). The Lord is incomparable. No one in the councils of heaven or on earth is like the "LORD God of hosts" (v. 8, RSV). He has great power and might, but He is also faithful and dependable.

God rules the raging sea and at creation overcame the sea dragon of chaos (Rahab in v. 10). He is the owner of heaven and earth because He made them. Tabor and Hermon are mountains created by God. The "festal shout" (v. 15, NRSV) was the congregational response. "Horn" in verse 17 is a symbol of strength. The king was God's "shield" to protect His people (v. 18).

The Davidic Covenant

God's covenant with Abraham and with Israel found its special climax in God's covenant with David (2 Sam. 23:5; cp. 7:12–16; 2 Chron. 13:5; Pss. 89:3–34; 132:12). God would establish the house of David to rule His people forever.

The Davidic covenant (89:19–37). Verse 3 refers to God's agreement with His servant, King David. Now the covenant is elaborated. It was God who gave David the crown and anointed him king (vv. 19–20).

The "faithful one" to whom God spoke in a vision was the prophet Nathan (v. 19; see 2 Sam. 7:4, 17). God promised David victory over his foes (vv. 22–23). The theme of God's faithfulness and love is reintroduced (v. 24). God promised to exalt David's strength ("horn," v. 24). His kingdom would extend from the Mediterranean Sea to the Euphrates River (v. 25). God would adopt David as His son and make him the mightiest king on earth (v. 27). His lineage would be established forever (v. 29). David's descendants must obey God's law. If they failed to do so, God would punish them, but He would never quit loving them (vv. 32–33).

Has God forsaken His covenant? (89:38–51). The Davidic king was defeated in battle. His conquest was most humiliating. He lost his crown and throne. The city walls were breached. He was held up to scorn. His enemies triumphed. The king was prematurely old and filled with shame.

In a royal lament the king asked, "How long will your wrath burn like fire?" (v. 46). The psalmist appealed again to the steadfast love and faithfulness of God (v. 49). These were the nation's hope. These terms occur five and seven times in the psalm.

Verse 52 is a doxology to Book III of the Psalms, not part of Psalm 89.

■ *The Davidic king was defeated in battle. His*
■ *conquest was most humiliating. He lost his*
■ *crown and throne. The city walls were*
■ *breached. The king lamented, How long will*
■ *God's wrath burn?*

GUIDING QUESTION

What were the essentials of the Davidic covenant?

Background: The situation that underlies this psalm is not identified in detail by the psalmist. He contemplated the transitory character of mankind's existence, and asked, Why does the life of humans pass away so suddenly? His psalm is titled a "Prayer of Moses, the man of God." Its similarity to Deuteronomy 33 is noticeable.

PSALM 90: GOD IS ETERNAL—MANKIND IS MORTAL

Theme: God's eternity and mankind's mortality

Reader insights: A wisdom song and a community lament

PSALM SUMMARY

God's eternity and man's transience (90:1–12). The opening line sets the tone of faith. The psalmist celebrated God's eternity, which predates creation itself. The mountains are considered the oldest part of the earth. The psalmist compared creation to birth (v. 2).

It is God who turns man back to dust (v. 3; Gen. 2:7; 3:19). We are always measuring time, but to God a thousand years is equal to only part of one night (v. 4). The psalmist described life as a sudden storm that sweeps away a hut or tent, bringing a person's life to a swift and sudden end. It's like a dream which vanishes on waking. Or, life is like grass which flourishes in the morning but fades and withers by evening because of the scorching Middle Eastern heat.

Death comes as a consequence of sin. (vv. 7–9; Rom. 6:23). If we are fortunate and strong, we may live for seventy or eighty years. This must have been exceptional in a time when the life expectancy was half that. But even eighty years is not long enough—and they are filled with "trouble and sorrow" (v. 10). The important thing is for people to live wisely and well, with a sense of purpose (v. 12).

A prayer for God's blessings (90:13–17). The people asked for divine favor that their short lives might have meaning. They pleaded for joy and for God to "establish the work of our hands for us" (v. 17).

- The psalmist began by celebrating God's eternity. He then contrasted the brevity of human life, using the metaphors of a swift flood and grass. The reason for death and the shortness of our earthly lives is sin. The people asked God's blessing on their lives, that their time spent on this earth will have meaning.

GUIDING QUESTION
What three metaphors did the psalmist use to describe the brevity of human life (vv. 5–6)?

Background: This eloquent poem was a dramatic conversation used in worship. The first two verses were given by the worship leader. They stated the theme. Next, the chorus or congregation responded (vv. 3–13). Finally, we have an oracle, read by a prophet, which represented God's promise of His presence (vv. 14–16).

PSALM 91: PROMISE OF GOD'S PROTECTION

Theme: Those who trust in God enjoy His protection.

Reader insights: A wisdom song and an oracle psalm

PSALM SUMMARY
The theme (91:1–2). God protects the person who cleaves to Him in love. This section contains four different Hebrew names for deity: the Most High, the Almighty, the Lord, and God.

God's "shelter" and "shadow" are ways of describing His protection. The metaphor used here is the shadow of His wings, like a mother bird guarding her young (v. 4).

The response (91:3–13). Next, the choir listed the ways in which God protects those who depend on Him. The "fowler's snare" represents man-made trouble, while "pestilence" may stand for dangers from nature. God gives protection to His own, even in battle (v. 7).

Satan tried to misapply verse 11 when he tempted Jesus (Luke 4:10–11).

God speaks (91:14–16). The oracle confirms the promise of divine protection. It begins by saying: "Because he cleaves to me in love" (v. 14, RSV). God promised deliverance, an answer to His prayers (v. 15), and His presence in times of trouble. He also held out the hope of honor and long life (v. 16).

This psalm is not an excuse for arrogance. That is the kind of idea that comes from the devil. It speaks of faith that makes us feel secure in the presence of the Father.

- *God protects the person who cleaves to Him*
- *in love. The psalmist provided four different*
- *names for God to describe His ways of pro-*
- *tecting us. The choir listed the ways in*
- *which God protects those who depend on*
- *Him. The oracle confirms the promise of*
- *divine protection. God promised deliver-*
- *ance, an answer to His prayers, and His*
- *presence in times of trouble.*

GUIDING QUESTION

What are the various threats from which the Lord delivers those who trust in Him?

PSALM 92: "IT IS GOOD TO GIVE THANKS"

- - - -

Background: This is a psalm of joy by a person who believes in God's providence and justice and has experienced it. The righteous have been rewarded and the wicked punished. This constitutes a call to praise. The psalm begins and ends with God.

Theme: Gratitude to God for His steadfast love and faithfulness

Reader insights: A hymn

PSALM SUMMARY

Introductory hymn (92:1–4). The psalmist's joy overflowed in a hymn of praise and thanksgiving. He pointed to the Lord's steadfast love and faithfulness. Believers can count on the Lord to keep His promises and to bless them. The psalmist praised God with musical instruments: the lute, harp, and lyre. He also sang for joy. His praise was continual—morning and night.

Destruction of the wicked (92:5–11). God's purposes and works are so great that sinners cannot understand them (vv. 5–6). Although the wicked grow like weeds, they will be cut down. Their doom is sure (v. 7).

The psalmist had been given strength "like that of a wild ox," and His enemies had been defeated (vv. 9–10). He had been anointed with the perfumed oil used on festive occasions. That is still another expression of his joy and praise.

Blessing of the righteous (92:12–15). Those who trust in God prosper. Using the metaphor of trees, the psalmist declared that "the righteous will flourish like a palm tree." And they are as stately as the cedars of Lebanon. Planted in the presence of the Lord, they flourish. Even in old age they are still vigorous and bear fruit.

The psalmist confessed his faith, saying: "The LORD . . . he is my Rock" (v. 15). The psalm is one of joyous gratitude to God.

- *The psalmist opened this hymn with praise*
- *and thanksgiving to God for His love and*
- *faithfulness. God's purposes confused the*
- *wicked. Their lives were characterized as*
- *weeds that are cut down. In contrast, the*
- *psalmist was given strength. Using trees as a*
- *metaphor, the psalmist declared that the*
- *righteous will be fruitful. Even in old age*
- *they retain their vigor and bear fruit.*

GUIDING QUESTION
The psalmist likened believers to trees. What lessons might we draw from his imagery?

PSALM 93: THE LORD IS KING

Theme: God is King of the universe.

Reader insights: A song of the Lord's reign

PSALM SUMMARY
The psalmist pictures the Almighty as "robed in majesty . . . [and] strength" (v. 1). He is king of the world that He established and controls. His is an everlasting kingdom (v. 2). The ultimate will of God will be realized with certainty.

The floods and storm of verses 3–4 are a favorite Hebrew symbol of chaos and trouble. At

Background: Because its language is archaic and its concepts ancient, this psalm was most likely composed at the time of the early kings. There are six enthronement psalms (47, 93, 96–99). This shortest psalm celebrates the kingship of God.

creation God showed Himself to be "mightier" than chaos and the deep. He is the God of peace and not confusion. He stills the storm as Jesus did on the Sea of Galilee.

The psalmist confessed his faith in the sovereign might of God. The Lord is both powerful and dependable. We can trust His word and His character (v. 5). Praise to the Lord, the Almighty, the King of creation! Celebrate His sovereignty. God is in control. We need not fear Him but may join in the psalmist's praise.

- *The psalmist pictured the Almighty as robed*
- *in majesty and strength. He is king of the*
- *world that He established and controls. The*
- *psalmist confessed his faith in the sovereign*
- *might of God.*

GUIDING QUESTION

What are the implications for daily living of the fact that the Lord reigns?

Background: The psalmist wrote this psalm within the context of moral chaos. Perversion of justice and violence among the people of God were triumphing. Improprieties controlled the communal life, and the rights of the people were being threatened.

PSALM 94: GOD OF VENGEANCE

Theme: The judgment of evildoers

Reader insights: A community lament and a song of trust

PSALM SUMMARY

"O Judge of the earth" (94:1–15). In the midst of the prevailing moral chaos, the psalmist appealed to God, the righteous Judge, for justice. The wicked are indicted in these verses.

They were proud and boastful. They crushed and oppressed others, especially the fatherless who had no one to defend them (v. 6). They were practical atheists as well (v. 7).

How foolish! Will the Creator who made the ear and eye be unable to hear or see? (Verse 9 is vivid poetry and a strong argument.) God knows the very thoughts of people—and their frailty (v. 11). Fortunate is the person whom God corrects, for he learns by being chastened (v. 12; see also Prov. 3:11–12; Job 5:17; Heb. 12:5–6). The psalmist was convinced that God will not forsake His own. Justice will be done (vv. 14–15).

The Lord stands up for us (94:16–23). God will judge the wicked; He will defend His own (vv. 16–17). God has kept the psalmist's foot from slipping in the past (v. 18). Thus, He can be trusted for the future. This assurance is a source of comfort to us as well as to the ancient poet (v. 19).

Wicked officials were not acting on God's orders or with His blessing (vv. 20–21). The psalmist trusted the Lord as his defense and place of safety (v. 22). God will deal decisively with the wicked in due course (v. 23). They will not continue to get away with their mischief. No one is exempt from moral law or immune to judgment. Many people have discovered this truth despite their assumptions to the contrary.

■ *In the midst of the prevailing chaos, the*
■ *psalmist appealed to God, the righteous*
■ *judge, for justice. The psalmist was con-*
■ *vinced that God will effect justice. Wicked*
■ *officials are not acting on God's orders or*
■ *with His blessing, and He will deal with them*
■ *in due course. In the meantime, God will*
■ *defend His own.*

GUIDING QUESTION

What will happen to leaders who do not act in accordance with God's ways?

Background: The psalmist wrote this psalm within the context of moral chaos, perversion of justice, and violence among the people of God. The three great teachings of Israel's faith are found in this psalm: (1) God is the Creator of the world and of mankind; (2) God redeemed His chosen people by the Exodus from Egypt; (3) therefore, they have a moral and ethical responsibility to live in obedience to His laws (Deut. 4:32–40).

PSALM 95: LISTEN TO HIS VOICE

Theme: A call to worship

Reader insights: An oracle psalm

PSALM SUMMARY

A hymn to God, the great King (95:1–7b). The hymn begins with a majestic call to worship (vv. 1–2). Note the importance of music and singing in Hebrew worship. Next, the psalmist celebrated the greatness of God as Creator. The Lord is "the great King above all gods" (v. 3). This does not mean that the psalmist believed in the existence of pagan deities. Rather, he was emphasizing the uniqueness of the one true God.

The deepest parts of the earth and the tallest peaks of the mountains belong to God. He made and owns both the sea and the dry land (vv. 4–5).

The worshipers in the Temple were told to kneel before the Lord. Normally, Jews stood to pray. Bowing was a sign of devotion—"He is our God and we are the people of his pasture, the flock under his care" (v. 7).

"Today, if you hear his voice" (95:7c–11). This section constitutes a call to hear and give heed to God's Word. At this point the psalm was probably recited by a cultic prophet as a word from the Lord. It is a warning: Do not repeat the hardhearted unbelief of your forefathers. They disgusted God and were doomed to wander in the wilderness for a generation (v. 10).

Those in the Temple when this hymn was sung were called to worship and warned about unbelief. If they disobeyed, they would forfeit their "rest" in the favor of the Lord (v. 11). The author of the Epistle to the Hebrews sounded this warning for Christians as well. Jesus requires obedience as well as the profession of our faith (see Luke 6:46–49).

■ *The psalmist began his hymn with a majestic*
■ *call to worship, and then celebrated the*
■ *greatness of God the Creator. He then issued*
■ *a call to hear and give heed to God's Word. It*
■ *is a warning to the people not to repeat the*
■ *hardhearted unbelief of their forefathers.*

GUIDING QUESTION

What three great teachings of Israel's faith do we find in this psalm?

Background: The Septuagint, the Greek translation of the Old Testament, identifies this psalm with the rebuilding of the Temple following the Babylonian Exile.

PSALM 96: THE LORD IS KING AND JUDGE

Theme: A call for all to worship the Lord

Reader insights: A hymn. Psalms 47, 93, and 96–99 celebrate God as sovereign King over all people. He judges the earth fairly. They are similar in thought to Isaiah 40–66. They show the kingdom of God in its past, present, and future tenses.

PSALM SUMMARY

"Sing to the LORD a new song" (96:1–6). The people at worship are invited to sing a new song—one in which God's salvation is proclaimed and His glory is declared to all nations (vv. 2–3). God is great and not to be compared to empty idols (vv. 4–5). He is the living God, Creator of both heaven and earth. Therefore, He is worthy of our worship and honor (v. 6). Pagan gods are impotent.

Worship the Lord, both men and nature (96:7–13). The psalmist invited his hearers to ascribe the glory due God's name (v. 7). They are encouraged to worship Him with their offerings (v. 8). This invitation is extended beyond Israel to all nations (v. 9).

The psalmist called on God's people to say throughout the world that God reigns. As surely as He establishes the world, one day evil will be banished and God will establish justice (v. 10). In a burst of poetic enthusiasm, the psalmist called on nature to join in the praise of God and His universal reign: Heavens and earth are to rejoice; the sea is to roar and the fields exult; even the trees are to "sing for joy" before the Lord (vv. 11–12).

- *The people at worship are invited to sing a*
- *song. They are not to compare God to empty*
- *idols, for He is the Creator and the*
- *all-powerful, living God. The psalmist*
- *invited his hearers to ascribe the glory due*
- *God's name, extending the invitation to all*
- *the earth. In a burst of poetic enthusiasm, the*
- *psalmist called on nature to join in the praise*
- *of God and His universal reign.*

GUIDING QUESTION
What difference does it make in our lives when we realize that God reigns?

PSALM 97: LORD OF LIGHT

Background: One of the key pictures in the psalm comes from God's visitation of His people as they gathered at Sinai (Exod. 19).

Theme: God's coming as the universal king

Reader insights: A song of the Lord's reign

PSALM SUMMARY
"The LORD reigns" (97:1–5). God has shown Himself to be sovereign over all creation, not only to Israel at special places like Sinai, but to all people. The heavens show God's righteousness to all people.

Fire is the symbol of both judgment and blessing in verses 3–4. Fire proceeds from God to punish and destroy evil. Yet the psalmist contended that "his lightning lights up the world." The earth trembles before its Maker, and "the mountains melt like wax" (v. 5).

Living God vs. empty idols (97:6–9). God reveals Himself in both creation and redemptive history. Still, there were those who worshiped graven images and "idols" (see Jer. 10:14). Despite divine revelation of the loving Father, people continue to give their highest loyalty to things less than God. The angels in heaven ("gods" in vv. 7*b*, 9*b*) know better. So do believers in Mount Zion and Judah. They rejoice in the Lord (v. 8). He is the exalted King over all the earth (v. 9).

The people of God (97:10–12). God loves, preserves, and delivers "his faithful ones" (v. 10). The psalmist has moved from the universal praise of God to the worship of God's covenant people.

"Light" is a symbol of divine blessing in this psalm (v. 11). "Light is shed" in the Hebrew text is literally "light is sown." God's influence is not static but growing and pervasive in the life of the believer. The psalmist admonished the people to rejoice and give thanks to the Lord (v. 12).

- *The Lord reigns, and He is the God of both*
- *judgment and blessing. But His presence is*
- *veiled and mysterious. No one fully sees and*
- *knows God except the Son of God. God reveals*
- *Himself in both creation and redemptive his-*
- *tory. He is the exalted King over all the earth.*
- *The psalmist moved from the universal praise*
- *of God to the worship of God's covenant peo-*
- *ple. The psalmist admonished the people to*
- *rejoice and give thanks to the Lord.*

GUIDING QUESTION

In verses 1–5, what picture did the psalmist paint of God's revelation of Himself?

PSALM 98: GOD AS VICTOR

- - - -

Background: This psalm is a variant of Psalm 96 and contains many of the same themes.

Theme: A call for all, including nature, to worship the Lord

Reader insights: A hymn. It is divided into three sections of three verses each.

PSALM SUMMARY

God's victory in the past (98:1–3). God's mighty acts on behalf of His people cause them to sing a new song (v. 1). God has granted victory and salvation, vindicating Israel in the eyes of their enemies and all nations (v. 3). God has kept His covenant promises to the nation. This calls forth their praise.

God is King in the present (98:4–6). The people, led by their musicians, are called on to join in the praise of God. Instrumental music accompanies their singing in praise of the Lord, the King (vv. 5–6).

God will judge with equity in the future (98:7–9). The world of nature, as well as of humanity, is invited to praise (v. 7b). The sea will roar, the rivers (floods) will "clap their hands," and the hills will "sing together for joy" at God's righteous judgment (see Ps. 96:11–13). When the kingdom comes completely, righteousness will prevail.

■ *God's mighty acts on behalf of His people*
■ *cause them to sing a new song. He has kept*
■ *His covenant promises to the nation. This*
■ *psalm is a song of victory.*
■ *The people, led by their musicians, are called*
■ *on to join in spontaneous praise of God. The*
■ *world of nature, as well as of humanity, is*
■ *invited to praise the God of creation.*

GUIDING QUESTION

What caused the people to sing a new song?

Background: This psalm was composed most likely at the time of the early kings.

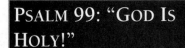

PSALM 99: "GOD IS HOLY!"

Theme: A call to worship renewed (a repeat of the themes of Pss. 93, 97)

Reader insights: A song of the Lord's reign

PSALM SUMMARY

"Footstool"

A footstool was a piece of furniture for resting one's feet, especially for a person seated on a throne. The footstool of King Tutankhamin of Egypt was carved with pictures of his enemies. Other Pharaohs were portrayed with their feet on their enemies' heads. The footstool thus became a symbol for dominion.

The mighty King (99:1–5). The psalmist called both people and nature to tremble and quake before the Lord (v. 1). "Tremble" means reverence for the Creator, not a cringing fear before a cruel deity. God's name is not to be taken lightly, but it is to be taken seriously (v. 3). His perfection inspires reverence on the part of His imperfect creation.

God loves justice, and so should His people (v. 4). The psalmist called the Temple in Jerusalem God's "footstool." Isaiah called the earth the Almighty's footstool (66:1).

Pardon and punishment (99:6–9). Although the Puritans made too much of God's punishment of evil, modern interpreters have come down on the side of divine love almost to the neglect of judgment. Here we see the psalmist strike a wise balance between these two activities of the Lord.

God strikes fear in those who do not believe but calls forth joy in those who place their trust in Him. Evildoers fear the Law with cause, but those who obey the Law have nothing to fear from it.

The psalmist referred to Moses, Aaron, and Samuel as "priests" (v. 6). Priests represented the people before God. They prayed to Him and He answered, revealing His will for the nation by giving His law ("statutes," v. 7).

The psalm concludes with the chorus (v. 9), which may have been sung by the choir.

■ *The psalmist called both people and nature*
■ *to revere God. God strikes fear in those who*
■ *do not believe but calls forth joy in those who*
■ *place their trust in Him. Evildoers fear the*
■ *Law with cause, but those who obey the Law*
■ *have nothing to fear from it.*

GUIDING QUESTION

What did the psalmist mean with his use of the term *footstool?*

Background:
Mankind is called to thanksgiving, to celebrate God as Creator and King. We may imagine a procession of worshipers approaching Jerusalem with its Temple gleaming in the sun. They sang the first three verses of Psalm 100 at the city gates. From within the Temple courtyard the choir answered antiphonally with verses 4–5.

PSALM 100: INVITATION TO PRAISE

Theme: A call to worship

Reader insights: A processional hymn

PSALM SUMMARY

Joy in God (100:1–3). The Lord alone is God. He is one (Deut. 6:4). God is the Creator who made us. There are no self-made persons. God is our Shepherd or pastor.

He knows us and gives Himself for us. God is good and completely dependable. The psalmist beautifully stated the reason for our worship in verse 5: "His love endures forever; his faithfulness continues through all generations."

Imperatives of praise—how we worship (100:4–5). The grammatical elements of a text often provide valuable insights for its readers. The psalmist used the *imperative* to appeal to his readers. An *imperative* is an appeal to one's will. It is a call to a specific action. Here, using a series of imperatives, the psalmist exhorts the worshipers (RSV):

- *shout*—we are to "make a joyful noise to the LORD, all the lands!"
- *worship*—we are to "serve the LORD with gladness!"
- *come*—we are to "come into his presence with singing!"
- *know*—we are to know God by our experience, that He is our Creator.
- *enter*—we are to "enter his gates with thanksgiving, and his courts with praise!"
- *give*—we are to give "thanks to him" and "bless his name!"

For more than twenty centuries both Jews and Christians have used this simple psalm in joyous worship of God.

- *The object of our worship is God, and God*
- *alone. Our joy is in Him because we know*
- *His character, anchored in His love and*
- *faithfulness. The psalmist appealed to his*
- *readers by exhorting them to participate in*
- *their worship of the true God. Worship is an*
- *interactive experience with God. It is an*
- *encounter with His presence and being.*

GUIDING QUESTION
How might this hymn have been used by ancient worshipers?

CHRIST IN THE PSALMS

One of the most controversial questions facing interpreters of the Book of Psalms is how to understand the many references to the "king" or "anointed one" (Hebrew *Messiah*). Do these references speak of a human king of ancient Israel or point ahead to Jesus as the ideal King and Messiah?

The biblical writers wrote of real-life persons and situations. The king played a most prominent role in ancient Israel's national life. More than sixty references in the Psalms highlight the king's prestige. The original readers of the Psalms naturally understood that these references spoke of the human king, whose role was so very important in their day-to-day existence. Because the basic meaning of any text is what the author intended the original audience to understand, "king" in the Psalms refers primarily to a human king of ancient Israel.

It may be possible for references to the "king" or "anointed one" to speak of both a human king and point ahead to Jesus as the ideal One.

The only clear passage that describes a human king in its Old Testament context who is seen as the ideal messianic King in a subsequent text is Psalm 2 (Heb. 1:5 treats this psalm as explicitly messianic). Thus, the human king in Psalm 2 functioned as a type, that is, one who had significance in his own historical setting but who also served as a divinely ordained foreshadowing of someone in later biblical revelation.

Generally speaking, references to the king in Psalms speak of the human king in the biblical writer's time. Occasionally, reference to the king was originally understood as a human king but later applied to the ideal Messiah. In one psalm (Ps. 110) the king can mean none other than the ideal messianic King of kings.

The superscription of Psalm 110 portrays it as Davidic. Surprisingly, the first verse speaks of David's successor as his lord. In ancient Israel this was inconceivable. David was the greatest king, the standard by which his successors were measured. Early in Israel's history this passage was understood as a prophecy of the coming Messiah. Jesus interpreted Psalm 110:1 in this way in a dispute with the Pharisees (Matt. 22:41–55; Mark 12:35–37; Luke 20:41–44). Jesus' riddle—if "David himself calls him 'Lord,' how [then] can he be his son?"—captures the mystery of the incarnation. Jesus is the Son of David but also more than David's son (Rom. 1:3–4).

(Taken from *Holman Bible Handbook*, p. 340.)

VENGEANCE AND VINDICATION

Sensitive readers of the Psalms have long been troubled by the harsh expression of vengeance uttered by psalmists, often attributed to David himself. Take for example these statements:

• "Break the arm of the wicked and evil man: call him to account for his wickedness" (Ps. 10:15);

• "Let the wicked be put to shame and lie silent in the grave" (Ps. 31:17); and

• "The righteous will be glad when they are avenged, when they bathe their feet in the blood of the wicked" (Ps. 58:10).

Such unloving statements raise serious ethical questions about the vindictive spirit reflected in these statements. Other prominent curses are found in Psalms 3:7; 5:10; 28:4; 35; 40:14–15; 55; 69; 79; 109; 137; 139:19–22; 140:9–10. Attempts to explain such fierce expressions fall into several categories.

First, some think that these curses only reflect the humanity of the author expressing his deepest desires for vindication when wronged by the wicked.

Thus, he was reflecting a lower standard of morality than that found in the New Testament. This explanation does not adequately account for the fact that the verses in which these curses occur are inspired by the very God who taught the virtue of turning the other cheek.

We must also recognize that 1 Samuel portrays David in a very different light. Although provoked almost beyond imagination, David did not respond vengefully but by tolerance and patience. The occasions on which David refused to kill his mortal enemy Saul provide eloquent testimony to this. Furthermore, Leviticus 19:18 forbids any attempt to exact vengeance against personal enemies, arguing against interpreting these curses as personal vendettas.

Second, another explanation sees the curses as only predictions of the enemy's ruin rather than as expressions of the psalmist's desire that the enemy meet an unhappy end. But Psalm 59 is clearly a prayer to God in which the psalmist asks God to wreak havoc on his enemies.

A plausible understanding of these difficult sayings must take account of the significant role enemies play in the Book of Psalms. Their presence goes far beyond the relatively limited number of psalms that curse the psalmist's enemies. The psalmists were often kings or represented the king in some official capacity. God mandated Israel's king to rule over God's covenant people in order to safeguard them and all God had promised to do through them.

Thus, any threat to God's people was also a threat to the very promise of God. In this unique situation, to oppose the God-anointed king was to oppose God Himself. So the king/psalmist prayed that God would judge those evildoers who intended to hinder the work of God, desiring that God and His work on earth would be vindicated.

Because of the unique position held by the king as God's anointed, he represented God's will in a measure unlike that of anyone today. For this reason believers today must not pray curses, for they are not in a position like that of the king/psalmist in ancient Israel.
(Taken from *Holman Bible Handbook*, p. 335.)

The following list is a collection of the sources used for this volume. All are from Broadman & Holman's list of published reference resources. They accommodate the reader's need for more specific information and/or for an expanded treatment of *Psalms,* vol. 2. These works will greatly aid in the reader's study, teaching, and presentation of the Psalms. The accompanying annotations can be helpful in guiding the reader to the proper resources.

Cate, Robert L. *An Introduction to the Old Testament and Its Study.* A scholarly treatment of Old Testament issues and topics. The author deals with history and various schools of thought. He presents his material in such a way that the reader can grasp the content of the Old Testament and come to view it as a book of faith.

Holman Bible Dictionary. An exhaustive, alphabetically arranged resource of Bible-related subjects. An excellent tool of definitions and other information on the people, places, things, and events of the Bible.

Holman Bible Handbook, pp. 323-50. A comprehensive treatment that offers outlines, commentary on key themes and sections, and full-color photos, illustrations, charts, and maps. Provides an accent on the broader theological teachings.

Holman Book of Biblical Charts, Maps, and Reconstructions. A colorful, visual collection of charts, maps, and reconstructions, These well-designed tools are invaluable to the study of the Bible.

McEachern, Alton H. *Psalms* (Layman's Bible Book Commentary, vol. 8). A popular-level treatment of the Psalms. This easy-to-use volume provides a relevant and practical perspective for the reader. *Shepherd's Notes—Psalms 51–100* has drawn heavily on many of the outlines from Dr. McEachern's volume.